The Cosmos, Ascension and 'The Golden Keys' from Melchizedek

The Cosmos, Ascension and 'The Golden Keys' from Melchizedek

Copyright © Sarah Massiah 2018 All Rights Reserved

The rights of Sarah Massiah to be identified as the author of this work have been asserted in accordance with the Copyright, Designs and Patents Act 1988

All rights reserved. No part may be reproduced, adapted, stored in a retrieval system or transmitted by any means, electronic, mechanical, photocopying, or otherwise without the prior written permission of the author or publisher.

Spiderwize
Remus House
Coltsfoot Drive
Woodston
Peterborough
PE2 9BF

www.spiderwize.com

A CIP catalogue record for this book is available from the British Library.

The views expressed in this work are solely those of the author and do not necessarily reflect the views of the publisher, and the publisher hereby disclaims any responsibility for them.

ISBN: 978-1-912694-05-1
eBook ISBN: 978-1-912694-06-8

The Cosmos, Ascension and 'The Golden Keys' from Melchizedek

Channelled by Sarah Massiah

SPIDERWIZE
Peterborough UK
2018

For regular blogs and updates please visit -
www.master-key-system.com

Special Thanks

I would like to thank Damon Massiah for all the support in writing this book and for his belief in me and this work.

I would like to thank Susan Kennard, a great friend, teacher and healer for all her support and listening to the ditties contained within this book.

I give special thanks to Carol Stacey and the healing modality of Rahanni, that she helped integrate back into this realm.

Thanks to Philippa King for her clearing of blocks to success though her 'Soul Coding' programme. Please see useful websites at the back of the book.

I give thanks to my other friends and family members who have received treatments along the way.

I give thanks to my brother Simon Hampton for the web design and support.

I thank Gary Bennett for the marvellous front cover design.

I would also I would like to thank Jenny Do Carmo for her meticulous editing of this book.

I would like to thank Spiderwize Publications for making this possible and for their great support.

I give the greatest thanks to the Creator of all there is, and my dear friend Melchizedek who guided me daily in the writing of this book. I also thank the masters and angels and beings of light for their ongoing support.

Contents

Foreword 1

Chapter 1
Get Out the Cocoa 3

'In the beginning. A story that time forgot.' 4

Chapter 2
The Golden Order of Melchizedek 7

Chapter 3
Planetary Ascension 11

Chapter 4
Interplanetary Alignment and The Keys 19

Chapter 5
The Key Codes and The Keepers 27

Chapter 6
The Law of Abundance and The Keys 33

Chapter 7
Harmonic Resonance and The Keys 39

Chapter 8
The Laws of the Universe and Ascension 47

Chapter 9
Ascension and the Ascended Masters, ...67

Chapter 10
Angelic Realms and Other Such Marvels 77

Chapter 11
The Esoteric Realms and The War of the Worlds 85

Chapter 12
The Sacred Ceremonies and The Keys 91

Chapter 13
The Esoteric Realms, The Keys and The Higher Self 101

Chapter 14
The Power of Judgement, Enlightenment and The Keys 111

Chapter 15
Love and The Keys 119

Chapter 16
Inter-dimensional Timelines and The Keys and the Journey Back to The Higher Self 129

Chapter 17
Remarkable Misdeeds and The Keys 137

Chapter 18
Fear-Based Beliefs, The Keys and The Dark Night of the Soul 143

Chapter 19
Discernment, Choices and The Keys 151

Chapter 20
The Final Countdown and The Keys 157

Chapter 21
Marmite or Honey? 165

Useful Websites 170

Foreword

I begin with this foreword in the hope some of you will take the time to read of my journey. I certainly never envisaged that I would write a book within this lifetime, and certainly not a book that would be guided from up above.

Previous to this, I never predicted I would have become a nurse, or indeed worked within this profession for twenty years as I did. I was a traveller back in my youth, carefree and fancy free, seeking adventure and wishing to explore this world and the wonders in it. I started to awaken when travelling, but back in the reality of home life this quickly dissipated. I realise now this was how it was meant to be, as early awakening was not written in my soul's plan.

I did, however, gain knowledge that would aid me on the journey that I now find myself. I learnt about the traumas that many of us face within this realm. I learnt about compassion and endeavoured not to be judgemental, although I now realise that judgement of others runs in all of us, regardless of whether consciously perceived. I have worked with the very young, the old and the in between. I studied general nursing and started a career working with those whom had suffered head injuries and strokes, mainly young and in the prime of life, and so I guess I learnt not to take life for granted. I enjoyed the gift of health, although in my youth I could not always see what was staring me in the face!

I then moved onto taking a second degree, after being left with a young son, and so went on to study public health and aid young families. I had various roles within the community, including aiding the homeless within our society. I still have a strong passion to see societal structures change so that the many that are suffering may get the help they so dearly require. I spent the last five years working with teenage families and saw many develop into loving and compassionate parents, regardless of age and experiences.

Within my professional working life there became a sudden strong desire and need to learn about energy, and so I trained in Reiki healing with a beautiful soul. So, the journey of rediscovery began. I then completed other energy healing trainings and 'Sparkle to Success' training with my friend Susan Kennard. I went on to meet Carol Stacey who brought in Rahanni fifth-dimensional healing with the masters and angels. This is where I was reintroduced to my dear friend Melchizedek who brought me the teachings of this book. I went on to train to teach Rahanni with Susan, and we continue to teach together to this day. I believe Rahanni raises consciousness and takes those in receipt of the Attunement to form new understandings, as well as offering a beautiful healing modality.

During this time, I had a calling to undertake the Akashic record training. There was a rationale for this, as the keys are held within the great living library. Also, within the key ceremonies, access to the Akashic realm is useful, as old scripts and contracts are taken back by Source, so a new resonance and learning may be laid down. This is completed so that a soul remembers the lessons without the emotional pains.

It has not always been an easy ride back to discovery of whom I really am. It has had its twists and turns as many journeys do. Awakening is not always easy, as you question everything. I have come to believe that this is positive, as discernment is required in all areas of life. So, some of you reading this book may find it resonates and others may not. Follow your gut, I just bring this text so you may examine beliefs, emotions and responses. You may dismiss this text, or you may find it helps you on your journey. Whatever you feel, I wish you joy, happiness and peace as you walk through this lifetime of experience. Now to the first chapter.

Chapter 1
Get Out the Cocoa

You may be wondering why you need to 'get out the cocoa' when you read this book. A mug of hot cocoa heightens your senses, gives you comfort and stimulates certain areas in the brain. It gives you that feel good factor. This book intends to do all that and stimulate your sense of perception, activating cellular memories. This book is going to stretch your understanding of the realms of existence and the space-time continuum as you know it. It's going to push your current levels of understanding about your world, the cosmos and planetary star systems. So, sit back and enjoy the read and take from it what you will.

The story started many moons ago before the times of the prophets who walked the earth, before the creation of this planet itself. 'Source, Creator of All That Is' decided planets needed a structure. Something that locked them into dimensional timelines. These timelines can be described as complex energy patterns that expand and diminish as Creator beings journey through various planes of existence. To ensure safety within these timelines, special keys were produced, and codes were formulated. Ancient scriptures and teachings were downloaded into specific keys.

With all this sacred information and teachings held within the keys, it became paramount that the keys were kept safe. Keeping these keys safe came with great responsibility, as within the cosmos destruction and terror were commonplace.

'In the beginning. A story that time forgot.'

Source had begun the story of creation by creating six inner planets which resonated at high frequencies. They were full of life and the gifts of many suns. However, in the outer spheres, war was commonplace. The keys and codes also held the wisdom of creation of sentient beings in the inner realms. On each planet, in the inner spheres, many keys and codes were produced. These keys and codes were overseen by the 'Higher Order of Melchizedek.' Melchizedek had been created with all the qualities that Source God found so dear. Melchizedek was given many roles and helped to oversee peace and harmony on each of the six planets within the inner spheres.

As populations grew within the inner realms, Source decided that a 'living library' was a way of monitoring a soul's experience. Stories of a soul's journey were catalogued, and keepers of the inner realms' libraries were then appointed, so Source could make sense of sentient beings' actions.

Volunteers were then sought from all the six inner planets. They were asked to leave the safety of the inner realms and venture out into the unknown to set up living libraries on other planets they came across. Source had created outer planets further away from Source's light, so Source could learn through the mistakes of sentient beings. All sentient beings were given freewill.

It was then to become a vast living library that expanded across inner and outer realms. This library was held in a space-time continuum. The books and the keys were all held within the living library. Access to the keys was restricted and seen as a high privilege. A 'Keeper of the Keys' was appointed and overseen by Melchizedek. Gateways and vortexes as you know them were then created so the Keeper of the Keys could travel between dimensions. As the universes grew in size, more souls were sought to work in the great library.

Rights were reserved for souls with the correct attributes from the six-star seed planets within the inner realms, to work with the keys. These souls worked very closely with Melchizedek and were known to work under 'The Order of Melchizedek.' Specialist training and teachings were given to work with the keys. This was a sacred job, as a soul had to have reached a certain point in evolution to be considered for such a post. The beings recruited were known as the Keeper of the Keys. There was a hierarchy amongst the 'key keepers', as each key keeper knew the importance of each key. Those in training had to undergo vigorous tests. This role ensured no soul's knowledge was lost. The books and keys together linked a soul's experience, expression, lessons, downloads and infrastructure that made them unique.

There continued to be dramatic changes in the solar systems, and as the solar systems grew, the consciousness of Melchizedek also expanded to keep up with the changes. Over, *what you call time,* The Key Keepers of other galaxies became more competent and needed less advice on the running of their solar systems. Melchizedek was offered a role change by Source due to the wealth of knowledge gained. This role was to oversee ascending planets, although he continued to be the Grand Overseer on a multidimensional scale.

Manifesting Key Set
Infinite Possibilities

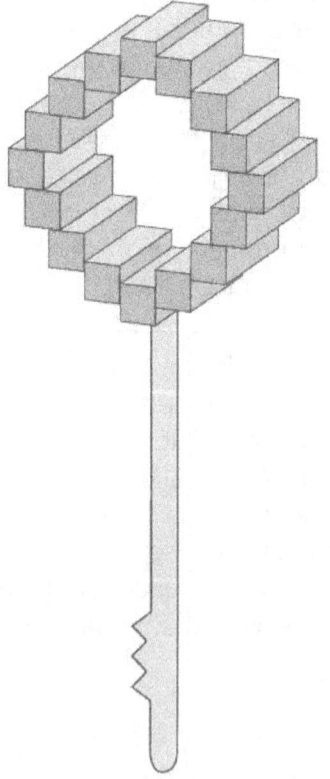

Infinite Possibilities
in Manifesting Key

Chapter 2
The Golden Order of Melchizedek

It has been noted that 'The Order of Melchizedek' began in the time of planetary expansion within the inner realms. Melchizedek was held in great reverence by Source as the Overseer of the inner planetary realms. Melchizedek was known at this time to bring great light, love and harmony to those residing in these realms. He held great authority, and his charismatic presence was felt by all he came in to contact with. He was also known for his wit and his love of life. He held a higher vibrational resonance than those within the inner planes. This is just the way Creator intended, as it had been predetermined that his role would expand. He was known as 'Creator of the peace' and no task was too menial, as Melchizedek led by example. Many sought his council and he was known to be a higher being of light. No one within the inner realms objected to this, as all knew the benefits of working as one group consciousness. Mistakes of Creator beings were still made at this time, and many sought the council of Melchizedek. There were sometimes quarrels and, although near to Source and the rapture of love, sometimes the sentient needed to be guided, to maintain the virtues and Universal Laws that Source had created.

Such virtues can be explained as universal properties, that combined, make up a sentient being's life force. That is to say, virtues are predetermined and contain attributes that hold certain ways of expressing the self and the way in which a being responds to an outside influence. If we examine the virtue of compassion, we will understand that it is a multifaceted phenomenon, which subdivides into many smaller aspects than the parts. For example, compassion has layers that encompass: 'trust that all things are equal', 'understanding of another's point of view' and 'certain rules and regulations, in order to maintain a sentient free will'. Such rules and regulations include allowing a sentient to make choices, even if they are deemed unfit at the time, as the idea here is that each sentient grows at their own pace. Compassion also includes the ability to view things through others' eyes, whilst maintaining detachment from the concept presented. Tolerance, truthfulness and trust are also embedded within the virtue of compassion and so virtues are complex, multi-layered attributes, as are the Universal Laws of the Universes.

The Law of Equality stipulates that all things are equal to the sum of its parts. Explanation of this can be determined if we examine a flower. A flower cannot grow without the right mediums in place. Light, food, water and certain molecular structures that sustain life. Its life force is the same as any other flower on this planet and as such equilibrium is maintained. If we examine this with human life form it becomes more complex. This is because sentient beings require all of the above, but also require all the virtues to be in place and correctly maintained in order for the Universal Law of Equality to be maintained at the higher vibrational level. Due to the phenomenon known as 'free will', a sentient requires an ability to maintain all the virtues in order for the Law of Equality to be maintained in its highest sense of the words. To gain a better understanding of this, the virtues and Laws of the Universe must be studied. It is, however, key to point out that this is what each sentient is aiming for, and even in the inner realms the virtues need to be attained and maintained.

Melchizedek's role here was to guide the souls, aiding maintenance of virtues and laws. As the universe grew into a multiverse, Melchizedek required help to maintain the status quo in the inner and outer spheres. We have already discussed the expanse of the living library and the notion of the Keeper of the Keys. It is under 'The Order of Melchizedek' and 'Orders of Melchizedek' that inner realm beings began to expand their consciousness, learn about the laws and the virtues and become great beings of wisdom throughout the multiverse. With Melchizedek at the reins, 'The Bringers of Light' were formulated, and all of this fed into the Creator's great plan. The plan of expansion of consciousness within the inner realms was underway, but in the outer realms things were far from perfect.

Melchizedek was the Overseer to the setting up of the great library and worked closely with the angelic realms to ensure a sentient's journey was catalogued correctly. Creator appointed a head of the great library who is known as 'The Gatekeeper of Time'; past, future and present. This light being holds the key to esoteric knowledge that can only be accessed by the Gatekeeper and Creator. Melchizedek worked with this great being of light and together they were able to ensure the great library ran efficiently. As the inner realms grew in population size, beings from the inner planets were asked to volunteer to work within the library halls. Here, they were taught how to catalogue and make sense of a sentient's journey and record all necessary points in order for that soul's growth to continue. As a soul returns to Creator's light in between incarnations, it is able to access the records, examine paths taken, choices made and journeys that were incomplete. It also enables the soul to look at progress made, others' stories and lessons where soul growth is required, and make new plans.

Those working under the 'The Order of Melchizedek' grew as the living library expanded across the realms. As the realms in the outer spheres grew, many more light beings were recruited to work alongside Melchizedek. Their roles varied, but included The Bringers of Light, The Key Keepers, The Overseers and The Healers. As previously discussed, there was a hierarchy amongst these groups, and different beings whom had attained a higher level of training and sentient experience were given roles within the roles in order to maintain a structure and aid others joining 'The Order.'

The light bringers held very important roles and worked very closely with Melchizedek. The light bringers have the innate ability to hold huge amounts of light from Source, and just standing in their presence enables sentient beings to expand their perceptions of the universe, cosmos and aspects of creation that are unfathomable to the human life form. The Bringers of Light are indeed known as ascended masters of the universe and as such they stand just under Melchizedek within the spiritual realms. Such bringers have ascended to the earthly realms and their influence continues to be felt by many. One such soul is known as Jeshua Ben Joseph who incarnated on earth. Such teachers incarnated to show the mass population how to bring in the God self. This can be described as arcane wisdom, long forgotten due to external influences surrounding the planet and lower vibrational fields that block such knowledge from being fully realised. It is in attainment of the God self that many aspects of creation are fully realised and acted upon, and sentient beings are able grow, not only on soul level but within their planetary form. The Bringers of Light work across many realms and are continuous multidimensional beings.

Many of the souls working under 'The Order of Melchizedek' have incarnated Earth at this time. We have mentioned Melchizedek's many roles and as The Key Keepers became more adept at the overseeing of different planetary systems, Melchizedek was requested to begin overseeing the aspect known as planetary ascension. Many realms have gone through such planetary adjustments and awakening of consciousness throughout creation. This concept is infinite as Creator expands in consciousness. Melchizedek's challenge within this concept is to keep all of the ascension processes running smoothly.

Chapter 3
Planetary Ascension

Ascension is an important and complex process, as souls need to ascend in conjunction with the planet. The energies need to be monitored precisely and atmospheres adjusted. Souls' energies also need to adjust. This is a big transition for sentient beings.

Ascension of souls at a vibrational level takes much adjustment. Souls ascend at different rates and times. This can be explained as the domino effect. Imagine a chain of standing dominoes that grows in size as each new domino is added or the soul expands. I'm sure many of us have built such a chain when in childhood.

As each sentient being raises vibration, the light quotient around them expands. This in turn affects each living organism as well as Mother Earth. If this occurs too quickly in group consciousness and frequencies rise too quickly it can have an opposite effect. The domino chain breaks down. It may halt or worse still collapse altogether. This can be catastrophic for a planet and the souls that reside there.

Some planets throughout the solar systems have been stuck in lower vibrational frequencies due to the collapse of the ascension process. This can cause chaos and destruction within these realms. A soul's journey is also disrupted, and new plans have to be made. This changes a soul's predetermined scripts, alters timelines and disrupts a soul's experience. Predetermined scripts can be described as lessons the soul came to experience. This does not take away from a soul's free will which is a Universal Law. The predetermined scripts have been carefully thought about by each soul waiting to return to a planet. This is done with much excitement, and at the time of planning the sentient seeks advice from other beings of light regarding the best way this may be achieved. You may be wondering if those on a darker vibrational journey may be offered the same opportunities. It can be said that they will. So, it must be acknowledged that in the realms and planets furthest away from the light, all are also given the same opportunity to grow and blossom into their God self. This may take many moons to complete, and due to the nature of infinity it matters not how long this takes. To step back into the light is about the lessons learnt along the way. It may be that some are stuck for 'eons of time', as you understand it. This is neither right or wrong, and any judgement upon this would be futile. Source made this so, and even at the point of conception of a soul, choices were given to the being and voluntary journeys were made with the love and understanding that a soul can return to the light at a time of choosing. Even in the darkest of places some light is able to get through. A soul that has travelled the dark path back to the light is in fact seen as a great teacher in other realms.

The way in which a soul learns each lesson is up to each sentient being. This choice is the way a soul expresses wishes and dreams. This can be fuelled by low vibrational energy or higher energetic vibrations. This explains how, at a multi-vibrational level, expanse occurs. Great wisdom is gained as Source expands in infrastructure, compassion and love for all things.

This disruption in ascension stagnates a soul's growth at a soul level. This means scripts have to be rewritten. Sometimes a soul's journey is cut short, so they can learn the lessons deemed appropriate for the soul's growth. They may reincarnate quickly on a different plane of existence, and this enables the multiverse to retain its ebb and flow. This ebb and flow can best be described as a perfect balance between timelines, energetic patterning, vibrational frequencies and the direct distribution of molecules within a given space at any one time.

So, it can be determined that the ascension process is quite complex. All these complexities must be taken into consideration. Ascension is fundamentally the Law of Expanse of Perception. Expanse in this perception can be correlated with the Universal Law of Abundance. Such abundance within the ascension process relates to the understanding that everything is interconnected. This is a complex process that interjects energetic patterning with the Creator of all things. Abundance is, therefore, a knowing deep within that there is always enough light to be evenly distributed around the ascending planet. This law and the deep knowing of abundance, lays within the cellular memory of each sentient being. The key for each sentient being is to maintain the flow of the vibrational shift from a lower to higher dimensional existence. It therefore must be said, 'that individuals must retain the belief there is plenty to go round.' The Law of Abundance will be examined in greater depth later.

The importance of earth's ascension cannot be underestimated. Planetary alignment around other planets must be correctly spaced in order to retain the ebb and flow of energies elsewhere in the solar system. All planets are interconnected. The raising of one planet affects all the other planets within a solar system. A solar system can be viewed as spheres within spheres. All planetary activity within a sphere affects all surrounding planets and star systems, and therefore changes inter-dimensional timelines.

Inter-dimensional timelines are constructed to lock planets and sentient beings in a space-time continuum that expands knowledge. During ascension this expanse is done at planetary and individual levels. As the planet and beings expand in consciousness, the quotient of light around them grows. As the light quotient rises, the planet is able to switch timelines that were previously locked. So, all within that planetary sphere move closer to the light of Source energy.

As this vibration rises, beings adapt and vibrational patterns that kept them trapped are released. These patterns are sent back to Source to be transmuted, and this darker transmuted energy is then filled with the rapture of love. These particles are then redistributed back to an individual or planet. And so, the ebb and flow of energy is retained and this positive light and energy that is sent back helps to maintain equilibrium.

The closer to the light the planet becomes, the more love and light touches the hearts of the sentient beings. This allows those sentient beings who have raised their vibration to aid others raise theirs. As light rises across the globe, more light in turn can reach the planet. This is important for the planet, as it too has been locked in lower vibrational energy.

Planets are able to absorb both light and dark. The further away from the light, the sludgier the lay lines. The clearer the lay lines, the less devastation is seen upon and within a planet's inner and outer eco-systems. This extends to outer dimensional grids. Such grids are placed around each planet, star and solar system. Again, within the darker and denser grids, energy stagnates and acts as a block to letting more love light in.

So why and when does a planet and its beings decide to ascend? This is written within the Harmonic Law. The Harmonic Law of evolution determines that at any given point in time, along the space-time continuum, enough of the sentient beings need to be in spiritual resonance. This can be determined as all sentient beings expressing the same thoughts, words and deeds. It's about coherence of energies sending out the same tonal frequencies. Tonal frequencies expressed as thoughts and sounds carry vibrational patterning. The higher the thought or sound, the easier it is for that thought or sound to blend into the universal sound of creation of life itself. So, the higher the thought or sound at a molecular level, the easier it is for positive energy to flow into a life, a planet, an atmosphere or a grid system.

At a vibrational level, the tonal frequencies act as an

energetic wave that aids movement of the timeline. It must be emphasised that this shift in timelines occurs across many millennia. When enough sentient beings evolve in consciousness, the timeline can dramatically shift. This is firmly locked down and anchored within the space-time continuum by a new set of patterning and grids. These grids have been restructured and cleared to allow in more light. All such grids across the cosmos are interconnected, all lead back to Source.

So, as the planet continues its vibrational shift and the ascension process continues, energies around the planet continue to fluctuate. The light quotient continues to grow as the sentients release beliefs, traumas and old stories held within. The ebb and flow then continues and equilibrium is maintained.

It has been discussed how ascension of a planet affects the star and solar systems around the planet. It also affects the multiverse, as all grids are interconnected so movement in one sphere increases potential for movement in another. This comes under the Law of Resonance, which encapsulates the theme of cause and effect.

Cause and effect has been discussed many times in the past, written about in many books. However, some of these texts fail to understand the key concept of vibration. In this context, the vibrational frequency of cause must first be scrutinised. The causal reason for many things happening upon a planet occurs when darker energies meet lighter energies. This causes a tug and pull between vibrational tones and this is where group consciousness becomes very important in the ascension process. As we discussed earlier, nothing can occur without a thought. That is how many new inventions occur upon a planet. The vibration of a thought must be kept as pure as possible. If many negative thoughts are projected at once, vibrations lower, despair sets in and the beings are then kept in a darker energy vibration. This can be seen in war torn areas, dictatorships and places where famine is commonplace. Many of you may be asking how such disaster can be overcome to aid planetary ascension. It is by thought and belief that these energies can disperse. Lighter thoughts have much more vibrational pull towards ending such chaos than any of you can possibly imagine at this time. It can therefore be determined that during the ascension process, positive thought forms must be sent to such areas on mass. The reason for including this in this book is to request that each reader send this vibrational thought out daily; make it part of your daily routine, just like brushing your teeth.

The effect of such projections must be seen to be believed, but if we remember the Law of Cause and Effect, which examines the inter-connectedness of all thoughts, it can be predetermined that great changes are possible. Ascension may be sped up for this to be achieved safely, all other constructs must be taken into account as previously determined. If this occurs too quickly, it may be catastrophic. Planetary healing must also be undertaken, and lay lines cleared, and for this to occur, sentient beings must be aware of the planet and the effects of their behaviour upon it. Out of date systems such as fossil fuels must be reviewed, and eco-friendly behaviours adopted. All those that are conscious must aid such changes. On a smaller scale, even the chemicals used in the home must be reviewed. This brings us back to the very salient point and Universal Law of Cause and Effect.

In the outer spheres, acceleration of ascension is carefully monitored and maintained. Positive energies projected into the planet's atmosphere help maintain the tug and pull of higher and lower vibrations. Around the full moon, an influx of positive energetic vibrations fills the atmosphere. These is adapted by the Law of Harmonic Resonance. That is to say, the distribution of molecular activity in the light frequency variant, over lower vibrational release, at the given time within the month when the moon becomes full. This enables the equilibrium to be maintained, avoiding disaster.

In conclusion of this complex process known as planetary

ascension, the relevant points must be taken into consideration. Ascension is a complex process full of adaptions. This includes adaptions in a sentient being's perceptions, thoughts, words and deeds. It also includes the releasing of stagnate thought forms and old stories that block the amount of love and light that a soul receives. That, in turn, affects the planet and its ability to release blocks held deep within. As more beings consciously send out higher vibrational thoughts, and as they let in more light, the grids that surround the planet clear and adapt. This in turn lets in more light and the vibrational frequencies along the outer dimensional grids begin to osculate. Equilibrium is maintained by the Law of Harmonic Resonance and carefully monitored through interplanetary and dimensional grids, all of which lead back to Source.

You may be wondering why any of this has any relevance to this book. This has been included so you may loosely understand the importance of your old stories that you hold onto, that no longer serve you or this planet. They in fact have held you trapped in a lower dimensional grid system. This was neither right nor wrong. However, the more of you that grow in consciousness, the quicker you can return to the light. A planet and its beings returning closer to the light is seen in the higher dimensions as a wonderful gift which many souls wish to be involved in.

Manifesting Key Set
Manifestations Powers

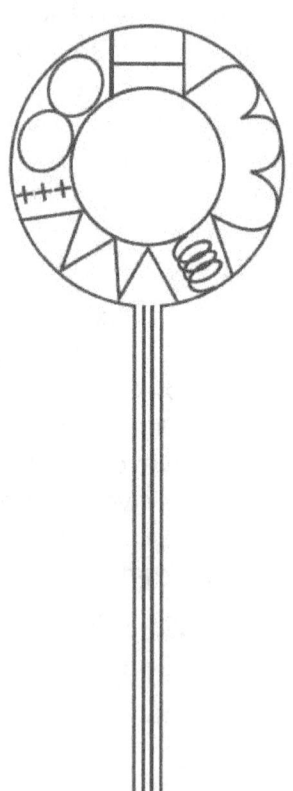

Unlock Gifts from Universe Key

Chapter 4

Interplanetary Alignment and The Keys

Interplanetary alignment and the keys play a major role in the ascension process. Differing keys unlock a soul's potential to expand in their energy field. Such keys also aid cosmic growth and interplanetary connections with other realms, clear up grid systems and are also used to prevent disastrous occurrences within eco-systems.

It is by the structure of the key and its components that each key is known. The story of the keys has been touched upon and their existence began when universal expansion occurred. Vaults that held the keys were produced as Creator decided interplanetary information held within specific keys needed to be kept safe. These vaults were held within the living library that holds souls' experience, lessons, misdemeanours and growth. A central vault was constructed.

Now, those of you reading this may imagine a vault as a dark, damp and dingy place. This is far from the truth. The vaults are reached by many external doorways that lead to many sections of the keys. The vaults hold rooms within rooms, and with the expansion of the multiverse, different key codes were produced to stop information being leaked between inter-connecting planets that may have jeopardised a planet's infrastructure, harmonic resonance and a being's way of life. Melchizedek's role at the time of creation of vaults, through to its expansion, was to make sure the key codes produced were in harmonic resonance with atmospheric pressures, the sentient being's abilities within the space-time continuum and maintaining the general ebb, flow and equilibrium that maintained balance within spheres. As discussed, spheres may be explained as planetary placement along a grid system that connects to the light. It was deemed as very important that spheres did not move and shift alignment, as the effects of this were seen throughout the multiverse. As the spheres grew, they needed to be locked into the dimensional grid systems and more Overseers of the keys were sought.

The key keepers were put through vigorous training, and The Key Keepers had to display a certain amount of aptitude in order to be given greater responsibility. Some key keepers fell at the first hurdle, although this was not deemed as a failure, as key keepers knew upon their initiation that certain skill sets were required. Such souls then continued their journey under The Order of Melchizedek and new, more fitting roles were sought. This included work within the great library, which was also deemed highly important.

It needs to be explained, just as is relevant today, all jobs should be viewed with the same reverence as others. It can be relayed as systems within systems, and if you examine worldly structures today, such as hospital systems, one could not run a hospital without the porter, chef or domestic. As within the Akashic realms, if one component collapses lots of records would be lost and a soul's journey interrupted. Key keepers undergoing the initiation process understood this concept of all working as a group collective for a better outcome for all. It is unfortunate that in lower planes of existence this is not fully understood by all, although no judgement is being made as this is the key to the soul's and planetary expanse, as discussed earlier.

The key keepers who did make it through initiation were then rigorously tested in the uses of each key. This included key sizing, colours, inscriptions, encodements and crystal and stone settings, and placements within given keys. Such study could take many eons, as the more planets joining the solar systems, the more keys and grids are produced.

Access to the external doors that lead to the vaults is

restricted on a need to know basis and there are now doors within doors that have many layers. Some smaller chambers within the vaults hold specific information about creation, the Laws of the Universe and minutiae detail on aspects of the soul, DNA patterning, resonance issues, the placement of lay lines and global, planetary and universal grid systems. It may defy your belief systems that such specific knowledge may be maintained within a key. You may even be asking right now why there is a need to do so. That comes back to an explanation about creation itself.

Creation is a multifaceted concept which defies understanding, logic and pontification of the human mind. For creation itself to continue, molecular structures need to be precisely measured, retaining the core essence of that part of creation. Within the key codes, such structures are retained. This ensures the key that holds the codes may be re examined at a later date and adjusted as Creator feels fit. This is normally done at times of change within an infrastructure of a planet, grid structure or sentient genetic encodements. Creator has made this so, as evolutionary concepts need to be maintained, monitored and adjustments catalogued. This is done in order to aid creations yet to be determined, and as a memoir of evolutionary potentials at any given time.

This can be seen if we examine the first created keys. They contained just five key concepts that held the essence of infinite possibilities concerning infrastructures on the inner realms. This included positioning of planets and the planetary alignment along the grid systems that had been laid down to anchor them into specific timelines. The alignment of the inner planets was the key to maintaining the infrastructure and status quo. Disrupted alignment meant the loss of sentient life within the inner realms. Imploding matter from the disruption of interplanetary alignment wreaked havoc in the early years of creation and exact mathematical calculations were then deemed necessary to maintain alignment across the grids.

And so, the earliest of keys were created so Creator could retain information on inner and outer planetary alignment.

As Creator loved all of creation within the inner realms and wished no information should ever be lost that may affect sentient journeys, such inscriptions were placed within the keys. Source had created many sentient beings at this time and although the living library accounted for a soul's journey, it did not account for genetic encodements that constituted a life, and so the keys grew, and within the inner realms much of this knowledge was placed within certain keys.

Keys were coded through colourings, shapes and size in the early years. Later, some keys held specific inscriptions that enabled Creator to pool information on thought forms. Such keys were then used to aid a sentient who had become trapped in certain beliefs and behavioural patterning to release theses ideologies by unlocking such entrapments held deep within DNA. This occurrence comes under the Law of Cause and Effect. This law states that there must be a cause for mutations in genetic encodements to occur. If we look deeper into this concept, many strands of our DNA at this time in our evolution are switched off. This is not only due to the cells receptivity to certain internal forces, such as the emotional response to outer influences, but also due to the genetic patterning of our forefathers. So certain DNA strands are locked into encodements that do not serve the highest good of a sentient. Emotional triggers that kept this DNA locked and dormant may be restructured by ridding one's self of the emotional triggers that held a sentient back, so their response to an emotional situation may change. This can be done in many ways. However, the unlocking of DNA patterning is more complex. There are keys that hold perfection of certain DNA patterning and these keys may now be used within these times of ascension to help restructure dormant DNA strands and encodements. This lets in more light, purifying the cells' genetic structures and instigating great change in the molecular structure of a sentient's energy field. Such keys are to be seen as a gift from Creator and must be used with the upmost respect. Further information on these keys will be included later in this book.

Later in creation, keys were produced so key keepers could travel through dimensions as formerly established in the opening chapter. This enabled the correct set of keys to be used within a realm of existence. This interplanetary travel was necessary, as key keepers who were more adept could visit the outer realms and act as gatekeepers to ancient knowledge that may have been harmful to planetary existence. Why was this so, you may be wondering? This is due to the multifaceted ways in which Creator can be reached. Those on a lower vibrational path explore and make various attempts to disrupt the light quotient within a planetary sphere. There is no greater time for such lower vibrational energies to try to interrupt the light than within a time of expansion in group consciousness. Again, this comes back to cause and effect. The effect of planetary ascension cannot be underestimated and is felt across the multiverse. The vibrational shift in one sphere can cause a ripple effect throughout the universe and may even be felt amongst the very outer spheres where the darkest energies lie.

Those playing out darker energetic patterning are held there by fear. Such fear, as previously determined, is caused not only by a group consciousness that disables the light, but also the lay lines held within the planet itself. Grief, anger and anguish are commonly felt and spiral out of control. This can be seen in the energetic patterning, vibrations and grids seen around such a realm. Again, it must be acknowledged that no sentient is ever deemed lost by Creator and all treading this darker path are welcomed back into the light at their time of choosing without judgement of past actions. It must be emphasised that they may become great teachers and infinite possibilities may open to them later in their evolutionary path. It must be remembered for those of you who are awake, the fact is that life is eternal, endless and infinite, full of opportunities to expand in consciousness, however long this takes.

It is, however, within these darker spheres where the light cannot be reached that change is seen as objectionable, oppressive and disabling. Ascension of one planet, and the ripple effect of this, may cause great change to begin on another planet. Within these darker realms, technological advances may be common place and so inter-dimensional travel may be a possibility. It is not the objective of this book to examine such a possibility. It does however have to be acknowledged that such a possibility cannot be overlooked, and blocks may be laid down to try to halt or delay the ascension process. This causes great mirth on the inner realms as it is well known that darker vibrational patterning cannot affect those truly connected to the light. For this to occur, the correct emotional stimuli must be in place. That is to say that the sentient affected must be running old programmes of fear. Such programmes can run over many lifetimes and during the ascension process it is vital that such fears are released. At this time, all healers with second sight are required to pool their knowledge and the wisdoms they bring. This remains vital because as a sentient awakens to certain knowledge and seeks healing outside of the normal belief systems that are in place, questions will need to be answered. Those of you on the ascension journey do not understand the importance of the role you play. That is to say, for vibrational shifts of ascension to continue, old beliefs, fears and expressions need to be continuously released by the collective.

This draws us to the end of the chapter concerning the keys and interplanetary alignment, but first we must revisit The Key Keepers and their inter-dimensional travel. The key keepers are still as relevant today as they were eons ago. Certain key keepers volunteered to incarnate at times of ascension, so they could help bring this information through. This is true of many incarnated souls at this time who are on their own personal mission to aid this important time in the history of the planet. For many, the construct of the great living library and the internal keys and the keepers may be too much for you to fathom. It is requested you keep an open mind as the book progresses. This book calls for you to deeply ponder your beliefs and views about the world in which you live. This may, in fact, call you to debate if aspects of this book are true. The objective here is not only to reveal forgotten constructs, but to raise awareness and invite you to explore your perceptions about the multiverse and the reason for sentient life in all its forms.

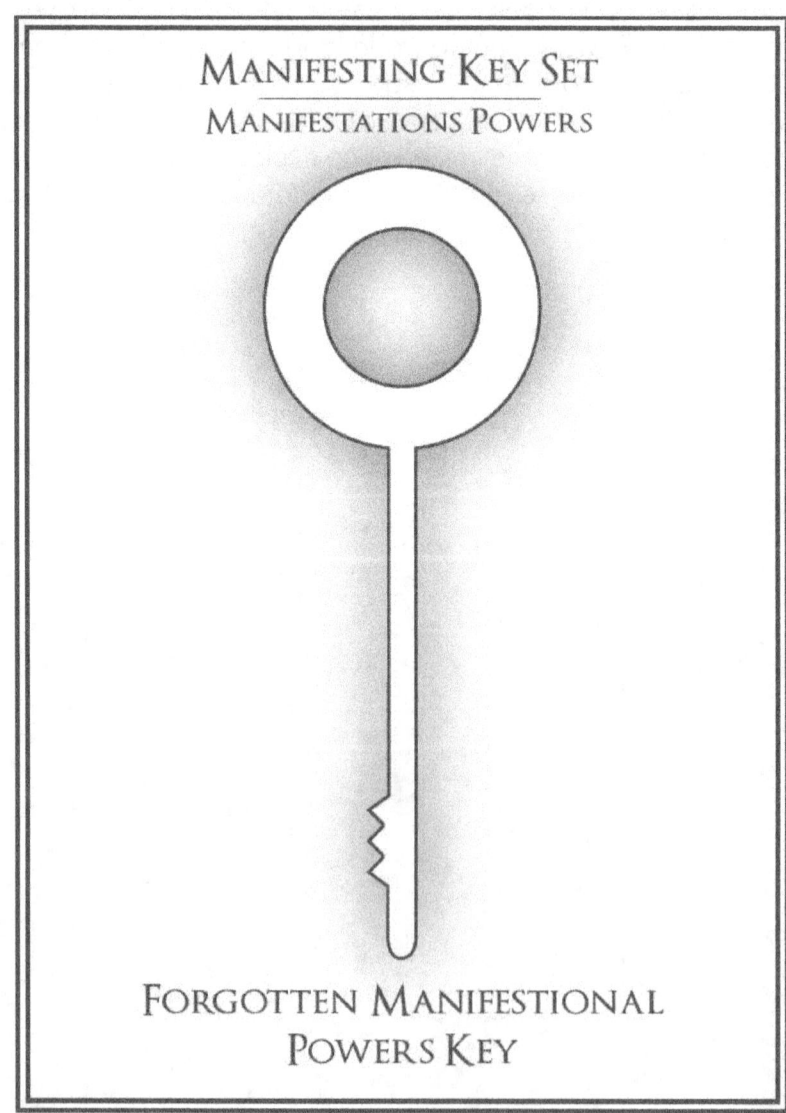

Chapter 5

The Key Codes and The Keepers

It has been said that interplanetary grid systems, certain inscriptions, ancient knowledge, fully functioning DNA patterning and positive emotional patterning has been downloaded into specific keys. This assists in the reconstruction of positive vibrations after negative, lower resonance energies have been removed during a key ceremony. The keys will now be examined in greater depth. We have touched on the first keys and the rationale behind these keys, and as we continue to explore the journey of the keys, great importance must be placed upon their power.

During certain periods of evolution, when the keys were taken out of the inner realms and The Key Keepers travelled inter-dimensionally through vortexes, certain mistakes were made. Such mistakes came at great cost to civilisations. Mistakes were made, and lessons were learnt. It must be emphasised that lessons continue to be learnt in respect of the keys and no judgement is made upon this. It is part of the ever-expanding cosmos and held within the laws themselves; 'for every action there is a reaction.' Actions and reactions must be viewed as growth of a soul, for without this construct no learning would in fact be possible.

The keys falling into the wrong hands can have catastrophic consequences and that is why the keys remain locked within the vaults within the living library. Only a privileged few are allowed into the inner most vaults. This was the way Source intended. It has been spoken before that Source loves all of creation, and as such this is held with great reverence and respect. Those that make it to key keepers are fully aware of the Law of Action and Reaction. This differs somewhat from the Law of Cause and Effect in as much as action is something that a sentient does, which causes a reaction to the soul groups they interacted with. Cause may be regarded with the understanding there is an outside influence that may impact the effect. Such outside influence may be described as the cause of the changes in atmospheric pressure. The use of aerosols globally affects the wind speeds and causes adverse reactions in the weather systems. That in turn, affects souls caught within a weather system. Their actions and reactions to this adversity in turn affects other souls around them. However, this is all tied up within the Universal Law of Cause and Effect as you know it at this time. The breaking of it into subparts is worth further investigation.

So, The Key Keepers underwent vigorous testing before the keys were taken out to other dimensions. During this time, Melchizedek again oversaw these expeditions. Vortexes or gateways were created to make this journeying possible and specific keys were produced to move quickly between the inner and esoteric realms (held within the space-time continuum) and out to the planets on the middle and outer sphere. Keys could only be activated to allow such travel if the key keeper had knowledge of all the component parts that unlocked these doorways. The loss of these keys remained in the back of all key keepers' minds. The loss of any one key would be cataclysmic and such loss will now be elaborated upon.

Here we journey into a story within a story. To set the scene, there was once a young key keeper who felt he had gained enough experience to exit out into the outer realms. This was many moons ago, and eons of time have since passed where this key keeper has attempted to make up for the actions that ensued. The thing that must be realised here, is that this young key keeper was 'green behind the gills', as they say, and all times past are just old stories. However, the key keeper ventured to a planet known in the outer spheres as 'Astonia.' This planet was filled with glistening streams that appeared iridescent in nature. The sky held a rainbow tinge and plant life was vibrant and glistened. There was beauty all around and the planet was blessed with the energy of the suns. The sentient beings here were tall and slender and they loved nothing more than tending to nature. Mostly the planet was full of love, and these sentients had evolved over time, as beings do, so there was little trouble on the planet.

Source decided it was time for this planet to move closer to the light, as many of the souls had reached a certain point in the evolutionary process. Melchizedek had been called in to oversee the proceedings and required volunteers to aid this ascension process. It is at this point that the young key keeper and the aids, known as key keepers' Companions, volunteered for this mission. The Key Keepers' Companions must now be duly noted. There are those that volunteer to aid this ascension process and have been given specific standing within the inner realms. They are old souls and although they have their own missions of raising the planet's vibration, healing work and light bearing to do, they understand the importance of the keys in planetary ascension. They were to incarnate on the planet of Astonia to aid the ascension process and were instructed in specific key use to aid the population to expand in consciousness, clear past issues and make the necessary changes in DNA.

These young beings of light knew that they would venture forth, incarnating in the outer realms to provide the tools for this to happen. The young key keeper may have been given the gift too early within the incarnation process on the planet of Astonia, and in doing so was not fully aware of the power held within the keys. Although guided by visionaries of that time, the key keeper held a certain rebellious streak. This should have been monitored more closely in the esoteric realms.

Due to youth and a lack of understanding of the power held within the keys, the young keeper made an error that cost the planet most dearly. The keys had been accessed by the usual esoteric channel, as the key keeper connects to Source energy and is then permitted to enter the living library. Certain key codes are utilised to access the great vaults of the keys, and this is where this young, inexperienced soul took some keys without understanding their true potential.

Some keys taken were to enhance the productiveness of the planet and the beings that resided there. However, three of the keys contained certain inscriptions that held the knowledge of the tides, tidal patterns and life within the seas. Those keys were taken as the young soul was curious as to what the keys were for.

One lazy afternoon, the young key keeper went for a stroll and ended up by one of the iridescent streams that permutated the planet. The young keeper had tried to use the keys taken but to no avail and on this particular day decided to call on the keys. Sitting by the stream, the young keeper decided to place the keys in the stream that ran by. This was an innocent act, however it activated certain codes held within the formation of the lay lines that ran beneath.

This changed the lay lines' structures, clearing stuck energy too quickly, and the rest is history as they say. Storm surges were seen across the planet and where there was once lush vegetation, only a barren landscape could be seen. The sky remained bathed with its rainbow beauty but the land beneath and the inhabitants suffered terrible losses.

You may be asking what happened to that young key keeper. Sadly, the soul returned to esoteric realms in the floods. Great changes were then made to the use of the keys during the ascension process and Melchizedek firmly holds the keys required for this process to be reinstated on planets. This is to ensure that such a disaster never occurs again and in the same way we began this chapter, we must be drawn back to the Universal Law of Cause and Effect and Action and Reaction.

It must, however, be perceived on a serious note that there are some keys being developed by the darker forces that try to diminish a soul's journey back to the light. If such a key should ever turn up in the esoteric sense, it should immediately be sent back to Creator's light. The darker forces use trickery and deceit as a way of instilling limiting beliefs to a sentient. They are very clever in their deceit, which also lures in beings with false expectations. All glittering keys are not gold. For all those partaking in healing work, to be forewarned is to be foretold. Temptations may be laid in front of you as the message of the keys spreads during this ascension time. We shall now briefly outline the rationale behind why it is important 'not to be led into temptation.'

Some of the darker keys have been placed within the cosmos as a trick and if utilised may impede healing, cause blocks in an energy field and have negative consequences for those receiving the key and those using the key. A tale will now be woven into this text to emphasise the importance of this story. During the ascension process on another planet, let's call it Hallow Earth, a group of empathetics stumbled across an old altar. They felt it would be a good idea to link with the energy of the place which they had stumbled across. Little were they to know that this site had been used by the darker forces to try to immobilise the ascension process. When connecting to this energy, they saw many keys floating within the energy field, many of which were gold and shiny. On connecting with certain keys, they saw that some keys wanted to be placed within each other's energy fields. Believing that this was a sacred site, they started to experiment with the keys. One of the group used the keys in another's third eye, and since that day the individual in question lost their second sight. The individual whom used the key then shut down theirs, as they felt guilty. Fighting between the group members took place, as they had picked up energy from one of the keys that held dark energy within its core. It is fair to say that many of their missions were compromised, and this turn of events had consequences in the esoteric realms. Many plans, stories and data had to be revisited, changed and new plans drawn up. A soul should call upon Melchizedek, Arch Angel Michael and the angels of light and know they are fully protected if they stumble across such a key and send it to Creator's light.

Within these fables we see a prime example of the consequence of lack of perception about the importance of actions and the consequences to all life forms. Take what you will from these tales, believe or disbelieve them, they remain, at the end of the day, a story within a story and if the Akashic records are to be believed, this action and reaction of the soul within the tales is simply that, a story, a catalogued account of what certain actions caused. Such negative stories are never good to hold in the energy field and Creator developed the library so this could be so. A journey is catalogued and recorded for the lessons to be learnt by the soul. All negative accounts are to be reviewed but not held on to like an old school shoe outgrown many years previously. It is within the Akashic realms that many of these old stories can be released and lessons learnt, new chapters made and healings completed.

The Keeper of the Keys, and those trained within this art, can bring great healing to an ascending planet at the correct time. That brings us back to chapter three, where we examined the ascension process. This is completed on mass to allow in more light and raise group consciousness, which in turn aid the vibrational shift between timelines.

Certain keys also aid the manifestation process. This comes under the Law of Abundance that will now be discussed in greater depth, as it is with abundance that shifts are made on a soul at planetary level. The Universal Law of Abundance is relevant for all planetary life, life in other realms and within the cosmos in general.

Chapter 6
The Law of Abundance and The Keys

Certain keys hold knowledge regarding the manifestation process. Such keys are helpful at a time of planetary shifts as they aid sentient beings to recall the gifts they incarnated with. There are three sets of keys which subdivide into three keys per set. They work hand in hand to promote such shifts in consciousness.

1. The Keys of Infinite Possibility – a multicoloured gemstone key that unlocks the potential to know life is infinite. Key two in the set unlocks the potential to know you are a Creator being and there are infinite possibilities when manifesting. The smaller key three, unlocks gifts of manifestation and lays down a new resonance to enable manifestations to occur more easily. It presents the infinite possibilities of the past, present and future.

2. The Keys of Manifestational Powers – The first key opens the door to becoming a Creator being. Remembering your powers of manifesting. The key is an opaque colour and emits a silver etheric glow. It differs from the previous key in the set of infinite possibilities in so much as it unlocks the powers that have been forgotten. The second key in the set resembles the first. It has, however, an etheric green glow, which when seen in the light appears clear but omits the green tinge from around the edges. This key unlocks specific DNA structures that allow manifestations to be felt and seen within a sentient energy field. This key enables the Creator being to attract what they are manifesting to them at greater speeds. The final key of this set holds specific inscriptions

and formulas that allow the sentient to be able to accept gifts from the universe. That is to say, as long as the gifts are for the highest good, it opens the sentient up to allow the gifts requested by the manifestation process into the energy field. This key is held in great reverence, as Source has downloaded specific formulas to allow blocks in the energy field to be dispersed. Such specific inscriptions have been put in place, as they will not allow negative thought forms and patterning to be attracted to a sentient. It is only gifts for the highest good that one can attract.

3. The Keys of Creational Forces — Key one within the third set, that of lack and limitation, has been formulated to clear lack and limitations in manifestational powers. This key clears the path for only the highest manifestations to occur. Lower energetic manifestations and negative thoughts are blocked from the manifestation process, and this key only allows manifesting powers to come into play if what is being manifested serves the higher purpose of self, others and society. Key two is a pretty little key, and its demure appearance must not be taken for granted, for this too is a powerful key. It unlocks limitations set around desires, and by that we mean the desires that you may have heard throughout the ages, such as 'money does not grow on trees' and other such limiting beliefs. It also aids limiting beliefs of not only wealth, but health and spiritual attainment. Key three unlocks limiting beliefs surrounding time frames, and by this it cuts down many hours spent in the manifestation process.

The first key within this set includes the key of lack and limitation. You may now, at this point, be questioning the first key within this set. It is very important to point out that this key, used correctly, removes blocks to lack and limitations that surround a soul in the lower sphere realms. It is occasionally used within the inner spheres, so to speak, to adjust a sentient's perception of the power of one. That is to say, the power of one thought, however fleeting, has the ability to disrupt the energy field, and within the inner planets all are well aware of this. In fact, all negative thoughts lead into group consciousness and as we explored, this can fuel the blocks we talked about, on a planetary scale, that halt and alter the light flow coming onto a planet. Such thoughts are placed there by many outward sources. If we examine the media for example, it must be pondered upon as to why negative stories have such draw to the mass population. That is to say, such stories of wars and famines hold a resonance of lower vibrational energy.

If we imagine a weeping willow growing in a boggy swamp with little light and drainage and nourishment from the soil, we see that the outside elements falter its growth, diminishing its ability to thrive and bogging it down. If, on the other hand, we picture the same tree planted in a lush open space next to a stream, with all the conditions that help it thrive, we see the tree expand exponentially into a lush and beautiful living creation. As this expanse occurs, we see nature drawn to its branches, and due to the outstanding beauty of the spot in which the tree grows, it attracts people to sit by the stream and enjoy its lushness. The energy given out by all enjoying the tree creates a positive energy around the place in which it grows. This positivity feeds in to the grid systems above and below, helping them clear limiting beliefs that have blocked the 'chi' or energetic flow. All the positive thoughts expressed by those sitting near or under the tree also feed in to the group consciousness of positivity, as love for the spot they sit in holds the highest vibrational pull. Love is, in fact, the highest vibration, and we will examine this in the following chapter, namely that of harmonic resonance.

We now discuss the power of the keys through a story. A story that many of you know well. The attention is drawn back to key points within this tale, as it is to remind all reading this to be careful what you wish for. You may, after having sessions with such keys for instance, decide you want to move to a new house and start the manifestation process of looking for a new abode. Again, we will now examine a story within a story.

There was once an old woman who lived in a shoe, she had so many children she didn't know what to do, so she manifested a mansion that met all her needs but forgot to ask it was out of the sea breeze. So, the wind came along and blew her house down, she was back in the shoe and felt like a clown. The next time she manifested her house, she crossed all the T's and produced a safe house. The moral of this tale is yet to be found, it lays in the tale that blew her house down. So, when using these gifts, the need to be sure is that you have crossed all the T's, when building your doors. Doors to the future and it's of future we speak, as manifesting lightly always ends in a leak. We wish you to know, within such a tale, all infinite possibilities are woven into this tale. We bring your attention back to key one, which makes you consider all stories are one. We ask that you therefore understand, that the tale which you weave must be carefully analysed, and with this take heed. So, when creating your future, we want you to know, make sure you're specific on what will follow. The universe provides for that which you wish, regardless of the specifics, unless stated in the wish. All that is given is for your highest good, it's the way which you get there that must not be misunderstood. So, on making your lists let it be known, cross all the T's and make sure there is no stone, left unturned. Consider the outcomes of this and of that and request help from the masters if you feel flat, as guidance is above you and can be brought down below. You may have followed your heart when creating the past or gone off on a whim, but future creating must be something within. Within both the heart space and your head you must use. All possibilities considered, before your wish list goes to bed, or a blizzard may swirl around your head. What is this bed of which we speak? It is calling for the agonising to cease. We request that you most carefully wish and then know it is done, and we granted your wish. It is in this knowing that all your dreams can come true, all of this careful planning helped the old women come out of the shoe. She released up her wishes and dreams, in the knowledge that they would soon be seen. So, on closing this story, we remind you to take heed, be careful what you wish for and don't do it with speed. Do not spend hours after with a crinkly brow, wondering when, why and how. Call on the masters and Source light so dear and know that your wishes will follow you here. Here in this space, that you call the moment of now, we wish you not to end up with that crinkly brow.

Once the recipients have received a full set of such keys, they are able to manifest at speed, as long as it is for the highest good of the soul and other sentient life. We draw your attention back to the fable of the old woman to remind you be careful what you wish for and make sure you are very specific; this includes about the outcome.

We conclude this chapter by stating that on receipt of these keys you will not rush out and win great fortunes or manifest great wealth, unless for the good of humanity. We add this, as we wish you all to dream big, manifest with loving intentions, with the intention of aiding others and the ascension process and never ever forget who you are! Remembering the manifestation process must be in harmonic resonance with vibrations of the love light, this concept shall now be explored.

Manifesting Key Set
Creational Forces

Clears Limit & Limitations Surrounding Time Constraints Key

Chapter 7

Harmonic Resonance and The Keys

The subject of harmonic resonance has been discussed and woven throughout this book. This will now be discussed in further detail. Harmonic resonance is observed throughout all the realms and on some spheres, such as the inner most planes, the tonal frequencies are that of a much higher vibration. Within these spheres they understand the importance of the intonation given to sounds. So, the language they speak is of higher vibrational patterning than that of the outer realms. 'Om' is the sound of all creation. To break this down further, if we examine the sound of Om and look at its vibrational frequency, we realise that it holds the highest vibrational patterning and sound. Om is the very sound of life force energy and vibrates throughout all realms and spheres. It is the crux of all things, the glue if you like, that holds all vibrational sounds together. Thus, the vibration of Om is seen in all of the grid systems and is vibrating within all planets.

To put this in terms you may understand, imagine a nerve cell that is surrounded by a myelin sheath that aids electrical impulses to travel at greater velocity. This is how the sound of Om is viewed and understood in the inner realms and Source created this sound to ensure that grid structures were locked in to dimensional timelines. The resonation of the sound Om is the sound of creation itself, because without this sound oscillating across all spheres, all grid systems would in fact collapse. Planets would not be able to maintain any life internally or within the atmospheres that surround them.

Sentient life would not exist, as this resonance is held within cellular structures of all beings and life forces.

Why is it important to contemplate the sound of Om, one might ask? It is within the structure of all things created by Source. This includes the keys presented to this planet at this time of planetary ascension. Each key holds a certain vibrational patterning that aids Source to bring in different vibrational structures and enables the sentient to clear up old beliefs, stories, patterning and codings that no longer serve a purpose. All keys have one common denominating factor and that is the vibration of Om which holds all the structures of the keys together and aids changes within the life force of those receiving the keys.

So, those in receipt of the keys during a ceremony, due to the nature of Om and the creational forces held within the keys, are able to lay down a new resonance. Resonance is described as a vibrational patterning that holds all the positive aspects of the creation of a species. This is the gift from Source. This gift cannot be underestimated. Once old patterning etc. has been removed, a new vibrant and dynamic structure can be laid down within the receiving sentient. That is to say, new codes can be introduced into the sentient energy field that attract a new vibrational frequency. We have already briefly discussed tonal vibrations and their resonance, and how within the inner realms the higher vibrational tonal patterning of the spoken or telepathic words cause a vibrational resonance that enables the sentient to deflect negative vibrational frequencies. As these planets are placed very much nearer to the vibration of Source, the sound of Om also keeps the planets locked into a harmonic resonance that cannot be fully understood on this plane of existence. To try to elaborate would be unsuccessful, however it is true to say that the vibration around the grid systems due to the tonal frequency of Om is much clearer within the inner realms than the outer spheres. To put this another way, it is as if the planets in the outer spheres would require a supersonic hearing aid to even get near to hearing the true sound and vibrational resonance of Om and even then, this hearing aid would be only forty percent productive.

The key point here, during the ascension process, is that the planet returns nearer to this pure vibrational essence. It may be pondered upon, as planets ascend nearer to Source, what occurs within the inner realms. The inner realms expand, allowing for more planets to join the harmonic resonance experienced closer to Source. Source watches with rapture as planets return to this resonance. This also allows other outer planets to move closer to Source. It is true to say that due to the nature of infinity, there will always be planets further from the light of Source. It again must be expressed that in this way all life force is maintained, as, if all planets were within the rapture of Source's love (the inner realms), there would be no ebb and flow. All things would stagnate, there would be no growth of souls or planets, and all infrastructures and grids would vegetate becoming inactive. So again, we say to you who are reading or hearing the words within this book, do not judge those further away from this inner realm resonance as without this phenomenon nothing would flow.

We now wish to discuss with you the harmonic convergence. Such convergences are, in part, vital when examining the ascension process. As we discussed, many of the sentient beings on a planet must be singing from the same sheet, so to speak. So, during the time of harmonic convergence all the positive intonations, utterances, telepathic thoughts and love converge within the grid systems and make it possible for a vibrational shift of grids. We have touched on this previously within the ascension chapter, that grids can be weighed down with negative vibrational patterning within the outer realms. This will now be explored in greater depth, as it is in your thoughts that the key lays. Thoughts hold a vibrational frequency. If you study the human brain, you will find that when a person is shouted at certain areas of the brain are switched off. This acts as a proactive defence against negative vibrations entering a sentient being's energy field. Much new research will be available in the future on this phenomenon, but today we will not explore the scientific rationale for this. It is simply a statement of fact. The fact is that your emotional responses greatly affect the ascension process, as the switching off of certain areas in the brain in fact deters the light quotient each of you are able to hold. The keys and the key ceremonies enable your responses to be adapted and change, so this switching off of cellular activity diminishes. Thus, more light is let through.

We have already, in the previous chapter, touched on the idea that vibrational shifts in sentient beings allows more light to filter into the plane of existence you find yourself on. We again remind you that this in turn affects the interplanetary grids, enabling them to clear blockages. So, it is requested that when you examine Jeshua's words, 'turn the other cheek', there was much to be said for this. Jeshua Ben Joseph came to show you the way to behave towards your fellow man. Unfortunately, this fell on deaf ears for the main part, but when we break down this announcement of truth, we see that if this can be done across the globe, much more light will be able to filter onto this planet. It is hard for you not to take attacks as a personal insult, but we say to you that this is in fact a gift. A gift from one soul to another to enable them to clear up, once and for all, all past insults you may be carrying. Such insults you will find in the Akashic libraries that hold the stories of your journeys on all planes of existence.

You may ask now about the inner plane beings and their stories. It is correct to say that they receive different challenges than you can comprehend here in this plane. They do, however, still have 'their crosses to bear' as you say. All sentient beings within the 'universes' grow from differing experiences, so what may be true in one realm may well affect sentient beings in another. It is their learnt response that sets them apart. Their cellular memories and DNA (deoxyribonucleic acid) make up that, in fact, enables them to resonate at higher vibrational levels.

We wish to impart that any vibrational healing you receive at this time can and will be beneficial to this planet during the ascension phases you find yourselves in. Pick and choose carefully. Follow your gut and intuition, as different healing modalities bring unique gifts to you. One gift that may be right for you at one point in time may not be right at another. Limiting yourselves to one modality would not serve the greater whole. It is the collective we refer back to, as with a sentient raising vibration it feeds back into the light quotient of the whole. Again, we remind you that this is enabling new grids to be laid down within your realm, and old grids to be shaken up, clearing denser energies. Aiding transformation and moving the planet from lower vibrational patterning to that of something much higher.

We have talked briefly about the dramatic changes down there on planet earth that you are all experiencing. Dramatic emotions and truths 'coming to light', as you say. Take time to examine that expression closely, as 'coming to light' holds great significance. 'Coming to light' is viewed by many within your realm as terrible injustices, but in this you are forgetting the soul contracts that those sentient beings made, in fact chose, before incarnating. In the utterance and belief of how terrible this is, you lower your vibrations. We say yes, suffering and hardships are terrible, but they come to show you, as societies, where adjustments need to be made. The collapse of monetary and banking systems, the demise of institutional structures that have held you back, the redefinition of the cosmos, all these things must be celebrated by those of you with an understanding of the bigger picture. That is to say, a new earth without suppression of sentient life, respect for others and their triumphs and perceived losses.

Perceived losses will be reviewed within this chapter, as it is within loss you make the most gains. Many will find this hard to comprehend at present, but if broken down into minute details we will understand that the gain from this is monumental. Again, a tale within a tale will be reviewed. Not by a poem this time, but by a deeply moving story of great losses. We wish you to examine the holocaust and previous wars and famines. We wish you to consider the horror of war. During periods of war generally, misguided souls revenge societies, killing many in their wake, driven by hate towards a section of society, greed or viewing others who are different from themselves as lowly life forms. It has to be said that these atrocities that have played out in your history there on earth, did however cause societal changes and different perceptions in thoughts throughout many lands. Think how you have moved within certain lands towards a more unified state. That is to say, if we view the atrocities of apartheid, which, incidentally, did not only affect South African soils as such atrocities occurred for many millennia in differing forms, we now see that this has enabled group shifts in many areas of society. Equality of all has been woven into many infrastructures within many mainstream societies. We understand that there is still much work to do on many of the issues your planet has faced, however, what we wish to stress is that if you examine the greater picture, much learning has come from such times in history. Without such learning throughout many centuries, many sentient beings would have stagnated in lower vibrational resonance. Many may find this hard to grasp, but it is of the bigger picture we speak, as it is the bigger picture in which your future lies.

It takes dramatic shifts in group consciousness for the planet to truly ascend, and for this to have become possible it has taken many, many millennia to accomplish. So, it is with great joy and celebrations within the cosmos and inner realms that your planet is ascending, as your planet holds the key to many possibilities upon other planets. We shall not digress into the ins and outs of this, but examples will now be shared. A prime example lies within the inner structures of your planet; it is of the lay lines we speak. Within the lay lines certain geometric codings are held that other realms are lacking within their grid systems. These geometric codes were laid down in the time of Atlantis and once reawakened are to be of great use to other realms of existence in lower dimensional planetary grids. All planets that hold such geometric encodements are able to raise their vibrational frequency within a shorter amount of time. In later years more will be spoken of this, but for now it suffices to say that many new discoveries about your solar system will come to light.

We wish to impart, for those of you interested in crop circles, many genetic encodements have been woven into your landscape and for those of you studying this phenomenon, this information may help you greatly when you finally piece together where they have been placed. These circles hold a certain resonance that, when activated correctly with Source, will enable lay lines to be much clearer and send out new vibrational frequencies that will enhance planetary activity upon your planet and within the hallowed earth. The planetary activity of which we speak includes greater production of crops that will sustain all life forms in an enhanced way. The encodements send out a light frequency that you cannot yet grasp that infuses the earth with a different monocular structure. Imagine if you will the earth from space, and imagine that the iridescent glow will be seen from above, emanating from your planet once such activations occur.

Back now to the harmonics. We hope that this chapter has explained a little more about the utterance of the spoken and unspoken word. We hope you gained a greater understanding about how this feeds into the group consciousness and how a group consciousness of positive thought forms enables ascension. We hope some of you reading this will be able to turn the other cheek, and we encourage you to clear as many old stories as possible so you omit a new awakened resonance, light and energetic patterning. We hope that in the future much of what is written here makes much more sense.

Sarah Massiah

We will now explore the Laws of the Universe, as it is in the laws that much of your future understanding lies.

Chapter 8
The Laws of the Universe and Ascension

Some laws have been touched on earlier and they are revisited within this book, as it is important to the Keeper of the Keys and those that follow that these are upheld, maintained and held with the greatest respect. As it is, within the laws much information is stored. They will now be reviewed in turn, in order to remind all holding this book of their importance. At this time, never before has such an insight been given into their significance, as will now be explained.

Each Universal Law is unique in its appearance, however together they hold great significance. They originated in the inner realms and they came about as the sentient beings required a structure, a code of conduct to follow, in which they could learn and grow. Without such structures, societal norms are not possible and no sentient from the inner, and now outer, realms would have anything to strive towards. Source upholds these values when creating and felt that all beings required this structure in order to maintain the ebb and flow of universal frequencies. Those further away from Source's light have to strive to uphold such laws and frequently break some aspects of them. There are, however, a handful of laws that cannot be broken and in the breaking of them the sentient incurs consequential lessons. Most sentient beings, even in the outer realms, understand that this is a fruitless exercise and so they are rarely broken. Those that do try however, are dealt with by Source, but that is not the point of this book. The first law of which we speak is the Law of Cause and Effect, and has been touched upon in previous chapters.

The Law of Cause and Effect:

Cause and effect has been discussed in some depth earlier, and we wish to remind you that nothing happens without a cause. We have determined that some causes are predetermined, chosen if you will, by the recipient. This is decided before incarnation. Let's say a soul decides it needs to learn about revenge, and before incarnating swaps a contract with another, as the other wishes to experience forgiveness. Whom do you think gains more from this? Let us tell you, all things are equal. Both those taking the revenge and those forgiving are learning an equally important lesson. The soul who is focused on revenging the other is, in fact, having the same lesson about forgiveness. In committing the act of revenge, the other soul may show them a new way of being, as instead of retaliating and trying to gain back control, they will walk away sending love and light. It may also be the case that the revenged soul retaliates, and then we see a cycle of negativity ensuing. Both souls will then repeat this patterning with other souls they come into contact with, until this lesson has been fully concluded. This, incidentally, may take many incarnations to complete.

The point here, if we review both outcomes, is that we see the effect. If we take scenario one, in which the person being revenged turns the other cheek, we will see a positive effect for each soul. As the revenger, they are made to consider why the person was able to walk away from this negative scenario. They may or may not have learnt the lesson, but the point is they are able to contemplate this, even if this is not evident on the surface. Even a fleeting thought can produce change the next time that the soul encounters a similar scenario. They may still act out on revenge, but it may be that they contemplate the outcome of doing this in a different way.

In scenario two we see revenge, and revenge acted out as the effect of an action. In this case, both parties experience what revenge feels like and both then contemplate, however briefly, the effect it had on themselves and the other, even if no positive outcome was outwardly seen by these actions. It is true to say, as previously discussed, that every thought, word, deed and, in fact, action has a consequence.

We are reminded of this if we look at group consciousness. Much research on earth has enabled discussions on the psychology of group actions. If you review certain theories, such as that of attachment, you will understand that the need for a sentient to belong is monumental. If you review many theorists on group dynamics, you will see that many groups have changed their opinion on the say so of another, sometimes to the detriment of the collective. Again, we see cause and effect within the group outcome.

On a grander scale we have discussed how negative scenarios are holding you back, and why reviewing this law is of prime importance. Such a law was introduced in order for Source to better understand the actions of sentient beings, how they respond, their emotions and how they perceive the realms in which they live. Source applauds you for being willing to volunteer for such experiences and understands the struggles many of you face. It must be pointed out that if there were no volunteers for such journeys, all would cease to be and so it is a mutually beneficial agreement.

Cause and effect was also written into the Universal Laws of Creation as it was important that each sentient was allowed to choose the outcome. As a sentient is part of Source and creation, there is no other way it could be. This was done out of love and respect for each sentient being, an individual cell of creation. Cause and effect therefore can be seen as destructive, but also must be viewed as constructive as both scenarios have the same outcome. They ensure creation keeps flowing, they ensure infinity continues, they ensure that nothing in the 'universes', and indeed in Source itself, stagnates.

We then draw your attention back to the ascension process and remind you that as you clear past responses that may not have had such favourable outcomes, you help to accelerate this phenomenon.

The Law of Abundance

The Law of Abundance has, for many, many years, been forgotten on your planet. Now you see countless books written about this topic. You can pick and choose those which resonate with you. Fundamentally, Source created this law as all sentient beings are seen as equal. This law was created so that no sentient is forgotten by Source, all have equal chances of creating the futures they wish.

On your planet much of this has, however, been occurring unconsciously. Let us review a scenario. Two farmers wish to plant more crops. In order to accomplish this, more land is required. Farmer one sits there worrying and moaning about his bad luck. Nothing good ever comes his way, it's pointless, useless, futile, as his crops do not thrive. In fact, his negativity spreads into his work and the living crops feel his anguish, negativity and general malaise. As we have pointed out, everything holds a vibration, a patterning if you will, and as such they can feel emotions at a vibrational level. The crops fail to thrive as this vibration deters them, the earth and the lay lines become heavy and sludgy. Farmer two, on the other hand, is of a happy disposition, sees the beauty in all things and loves creating healthy crops. The term 'singing while you work' comes to mind, and he is positive he can accomplish the task of gaining more land. He eventually does find himself with enough money to pursue his dream, and due to his beliefs that all is good in his world, the universe provides him with not only a new field, but a new home to boot. This is in part because he held a deep rooted belief that this would always be his destiny.

We have talked to you about the choices you made before incarnating on this plane, we must now explore the choices you make on this plane. We have spoken about how a thought, word or deed holds a frequency and ask you to re-examine your beliefs about your purpose and goals during this incarnation. No incarnation is ever lost; we wish to point out. Lessons, however trivial, have a monumental effect on timelines, as all build up into a total of the whole, and gains and triumphs cannot be underestimated. It is the detrimental patternings that resonate within many of you of which we now speak, as this is holding you back from reaching your full potential. The releasing of negative blocks and beliefs will aid you in coming into an understanding of who you truly are.

Source created this law as it is wished that all have equal opportunity to create marvellous lives during an incarnation. Within the denser realms this has not always been possible, as we have discussed many blocks and obstructions hold you back. Again, during the ascension period certain tools have been reintroduced to aid you clear beliefs. One such tool is held within 'The Keys from Melchizedek' and they come in a set of three. They aid the unlocking of creative potentials and clear past life events that have kept you locked into an unhealthy, shall we say, resonance. Such blocks are important for you to clear at this time, as when you create from a positive reference point, with an understanding of infinite potentials, you are able to allow in a greater amount of light. This is known to have a catalyst effect when viewing the greater picture, as all positivity feeds into the vibration of love, the resonance that is the universal Creator of all things.

The Universal Law of Creation

This law has often been viewed with some confusion. That is to say that not all have considered the concept of ebb and flow. Ebb and flow have been viewed from differing angles. It is the ebb we wish to first explore. Ebb, in worldly terms, means things move backwards in one direction. However, a multidimensional perspective is where we see the bigger picture. It is the negatively charged atoms that generate such a pull. They hold a denser atomical make up than the positively charged atomical make up we see in flow. That is to say, the pull between the negatively charged atoms and the positively charged atoms holds great importance, as without this constant state of flux all would stop, there would be no ebb and flow.

Such ebb and flow is seen through all walks of life. If we take the basic function of a cell, we would notice this ebb and flow. All living things have one thing in common; that ebb and flow can be seen. Within creation we also see this ebb and flow in thought processes as negatively charged thoughts hold a denser vibration than those that are positively charged. Again, in the time of ascension of a planet, we discuss this variance between the negatively charged matter and the lighter, positively charged matter, as light holds a higher electromagnetic pull than its denser counterpart. If we examine the lay line structures and grids we see around the planet, we notice those of higher vibrational resonance oscillate at a greater velocity. Again, we bring you back to the sound of Om, which requires further research within your realm. The correlation between this sound and the light quotient in any given space in time requires further investigation, as we again impart that this is the sound of creation. The glue, if you like, that enables all things to oscillate. The Law of Creation is, therefore, weaved into all laws and it has been stated that even the very dense and negative planets in the outermost spheres have some positively charged particles, as no life force would be able to exist if it was not so.

The Universal Law of Resonance

As already discussed, the Law of Resonance feeds back into the Law of Creation. The Law of Resonance states that all things, including thoughts, must have a vibrational rate. That is to say, the vibration of a thought or word holds certain reverberations and thus consequence. This is significant, as negatively charged words and thoughts all lead back to the group consciousness

lowering not only the individual's vibration, but that of the planet. If we take a swear word for example, we see this has a more negatively charged resonance than those words at the higher end of the scale. Love, for example, is one of the highest vibration words you find in your vocabulary. Without the Law of Resonance, the ebb and flow would also cease.

Let us review this concept by examining the consciousness of your pets. A dog treated with an unkind resonance will behave in a way that allows this resonance into its energy field. It will cower away from the aggressor or it may be more inclined to lash out and bite. If we look at a dog treated with love and respect, we will see that the dog is then able to more easily hold the resonance of the love it has been shown and behave accordingly. We also see this within the plant kingdom, as we have previously discussed. Crops can grow if the sentient expresses a higher resonance and positive thought process towards such life.

So, we bring you back once again to your thoughts, words, actions and deeds. The Law or Resonance is greatly understood upon the inner planes of existence and we would encourage you to bring this law into your modern-day education systems. Within the inner planes this is a given, and the use of the concept starts from the first days of incarnation. It is woven into the very fabric of life within and upon the planet, ensuring that grid systems upon and within remain as pure as possible. Again, we call those of you reading this to ponder on this beautiful Law of Resonance and those of you within the research, scientific and educational fields to pay it more attention. We ask those of you who are spiritually awake or awakening to clear your past traumas and become a clearer channel of light.

We will now ask you to examine your habits, as it is within detrimental habits that we see blocks in the light. Habits are formed due to your emotional responses to a given situation. Let's take alcohol. We can see that a sentient may have an addictive tendency towards the drink. This may be genetically brought in as a family trait. Such addiction may have begun in the life of 'Aunt Mary', three generations back, as she was beaten by her husband and worked all day till her hands were red raw and this had psychological implications. Part of her brain shut off and she felt she needed to escape from the atrocities she was facing. She found gin and began to join her husband in the local pub. You can imagine the scene, something that might have been depicted in great art works of the time, such as those of Henri de Toulouse-Lautrec. We then see that this energetic resonance was carried through the bloodlines and part of her cellular memories had been shut down in order to cope.

So, she went on to have four children and was heavily drinking at this time. The resonance of her cellular activity dictated that drinking was required to block emotional responses. Numb her, if you will. Two of her children became heavy drinkers, the other two did not. Why, you may ask, did only two take up this addictive patterning? We then say to you that their life experiences were less than great. One of her children found himself down the mines. His lungs deteriorated after a collapse of the walls where dust and inflammatory particles were found. He could no longer work as he did and he spent many a day in a bar drinking away his sorrows when money allowed.

The other son, who did not pick up this habit, went off to sea at an early age and had a life full of hard work and adventure. He had a drink but was reminded of his upbringing and so this triggered him to limit his alcohol consumption. Due to his happy disposition, he remained having a positive outlook, and therefore did not go down the same route as other family members. So here we see genetically it is possible to resonate with certain behaviours, and generations on this path may still resonate to some degree in the cellular memories that are unconsciously brought in. We discuss cellular memories within the Law of Resonance as cellular memories also hold vibrational patterning that may be of detriment. We have discussed the power of your thoughts; unconscious thoughts must be taken in to account.

At this time, it is important to review relationships between behaviours and your ancestral pasts. It is handy to clear such scenes within the Akashics, and Source is more than happy to oblige when this request is made. In doing this you are then able to bring in new resonance and we are happy to say the key is now back in service, including those of addictive patterning and a key that clears habits. More of this later. To conclude this law, we again ask you to examine all utterances, thoughts however fleeting, your actions and behaviours. Enough has been said on the rationale as to why, but needless to say, this will greatly aid the ascension process.

The Universal Law of Realisation

Not yet discussed on this realm, is the Law of Realisation. When a sentient is truly able to step into the light body, know their true identity and behave in a manner that befits such an understanding, then we can truly say that the sentient has evolved to higher dimensions of light. This is the Law of Realisation. Within this realm you call earth, this spiritual understanding had begun to be realised, pardon the pun. However, due to limitations this was not fully understood. The times of which we speak are the times known as Atlantis and Limeira. It is sufficient to say that there was much fighting between the elders in the later stages. We write this now in the hope that this will be avoided this time around, as the Golden Age of which you speak is upon you, albeit in the very early stages.

So, it is decided that at a certain point The Key to aid the elders will be introduced by the powers that be to diminish the chances of such a reoccurrence. We do wish you, however, as you continue on this ascension path, to gain a better understanding of this concept and law. There will be some books on the topic within your future, but for now we wish you to understand and take back your powers that have diminished due to lower vibrations you have found yourselves in. Again, woven through this text we remind you to clear up old baggage, as such stories no longer serve you. In discussing clearing such scripts we emphasise that no journey is ever forgotten, and it is the emotional responses you clear and not the lessons you learnt. Those are stored within the great living library under lock and key and no sentient has access to this information. It may at times be contemplated upon with a sentient's higher self, and guides Source if the need should arise, but that is a story for another book.

The Law of Reciprocity

The Law of Reciprocity has sometimes been discussed in other laws and if we review this we will see that all laws are interconnected. This law, however, also stands alone and if we look at all things in life we see all things are reciprocal. If we take the Law of Creation and the velocity between denser mass and lighter mass, we see such reciprocity. This is also seen throughout the plant and animal kingdoms. The soil in which a plant spreads its roots would not thrive without the medium of the soil and its nutrients. The soil would not survive without plant, as the soil relies on the plant to bring nutrients back into its composition.

We can also view reciprocity when we examine animal life relationships. A calf would not survive without the cow. The cow gains through the calf by the very fact it is nurturing its infant. Great love is normally shared in this way. Sentient beings also greatly require this phenomenon. If we take Bowlby's attachment theory, there is a reciprocal relationship between a parent and its young. The parent gains from the child, just as the child gains from the parent. However, sometimes this reciprocal relationship goes wrong, and we ask you now to examine why. Reciprocity is a fundamental requirement for life.

Such reciprocity is also in effect within the outer realms, although we see it in a very diluted form. There once was a dark lord whom wished to control all other sentient beings he came across. He used mind games to lull them into a false sense of security and then he used certain energetic techniques to distort their minds and get them to act out of character. Uprising became a norm within the area he lived and then this spread across the lands, as his knowledge was used to install fear into the masses. Those that did not agree with his rhetoric were destroyed and many beings went into hiding. This carried on for many millennia and the planet was full of strife.

A prefix to this occurrence was that the beings he tricked had a feeling that all was not well. They failed to follow their intuition, which they had the right to do as free will is a gift given to all sentient life, but they chose to ignore the warning signs. They believed that this reciprocal arrangement would serve them greatly, and in some ways it did. They too were taught how to control others and they felt all important and powerful. They lived like lords while masses perished. The moral of this tale is that reciprocity is still evident, as the dark lord had followers and the followers gained.

We have seen this in differing forms throughout your history, and we ask you now to review these happenings. Intuitively, we know deep within the correct pathways to take. Often this feeling has been blocked, as genetically it is brought in through ancestral lineage. On top of this, many have not correctly experienced reciprocity during their early years, due to parental upbringings. Another compounding fact is your educational systems that have thwarted this intuitive ability, and therefore many of you find yourselves within incorrect career choices. If we go higher than this we see government structures that do not serve the whole, and this needs to change. Great shakes ups are underway. If this did not occur there would be no transition to a higher dimensional existence.

We now bring you back to the Law of Reciprocity, as it is within this law that many of the answers can be found. For true reciprocity to occur, and by that we mean the light, right and most profound way possible, all must change their thought processes. Reciprocity begins in childhood, it is a learnt response to a given situation that in the inner realms comes from true love, not material, controlling and misunderstood gains. It comes from the heart field of the general population and all understand this law to its greatest extent. That is to say, if a young sentient falls off the correct path it is not abolished, shouted at, made to feel small. Those with the greater wisdom of elderly years understand what is needed, and that is to send love, to have patience, to spend time with the young sentient and review their options. Peers are brought in to love the sentient who is experiencing hardship and the general populous offers support to the family without judgement.

We shall also discuss the creation of a new life within the inner realms. This is carefully considered by the family and the community in which they live, as all know the importance of an incarnation. Timings are considered for this new soul to join their communities and careful pre-planning takes place. The elders give the new parents support and guidance and lessons are set up in order to aid this event. The lessons of which we speak include an in depth exploration of the Law of Reciprocity and this love for the new soul begins in the planning, enabling this soul to feel the love before the choice of parents is made.

We again bring you back to the choice, free will, if you like. All sentient beings are allowed such a choice, as all have predetermined lessons they wish to experience. Great thought is given to this in the esoteric realms. This also includes those that choose a darker path as they wish to learn about anger, control and abuse, for example. This may be hard for some reading this to comprehend. Again, we bring you back to the overwhelming point of ebb and flow. Reviewed in this way we come to an understanding that without such lessons, life itself would cease. Although atrocities cannot be ordained, there is always a risk that within the learning of such a lesson this may be a consequence. Such sentients on this journey are not judged within the esoteric realm, although their life review can be very hard to take, and they may spend a long time within this realm before they find themselves in another incarnation. As they progress along the continuum that we call incarnated life, we may see such a sentient becoming a great teacher to others whom have taken the same root. Enough of this. We digress. Back to early incarnation experience. We wish to inform you that we hope in the future that many new schools of thought will be available and those that are awake, so to speak, will evolve new projects. Projects that aid parents, no matter what their circumstance, to thrive and have loving reciprocal relationships. We hope The Healers will remove blocks to such ventures being possible. We hope more research is completed upon the effects of the Law of Reciprocity. And so, we 'endeth this lesson', and hope those reading this in certain professions are change agents for societal norms.

The Law of Compassion

The Law of Compassion is often what we see missing on your planet. Have you got compassion for all living things? Do you appreciate the beauty all around you? Even those in the inner cities can notice a flower, or the way the leaves rustle in the wind. Those that see no beauty are those who suffer and are suppressed; they do not have the basic requirements to survive, and we say to you, this will have to change. The future of your planet depends on this ability, for you, the awakened ones, coming to the aid of those less fortunate. It is all about perception of belief, and for these things to change perception of belief must come first.

That is why we now bring you back to the 'Key of Compassion', and those of you in receipt of this key will be able to see that compassion is a necessity in order to be instrumental in such changes within your realm. Back to the law that Source created within the inner realms, in order that they understand who they truly are. That, my friends, is part of creation, part of Source's rapture of love, part of the chi life force, an energetic resonance of creation. In love for all things, life force and creation, the true God self, can step forward. Sentient beings can truly feel the rapture of love, which is the essence of all cores.

Within the outer realms, again we see blockages to this realisation, as compassion is often waning. We can see this in most of your societies, as often people are left to fend for themselves on the streets. Children are left alone with no place to call home; food is scarce, even though there is plenty. We remind you that great changes will be necessary to alter many of these phenomena. The time of change is upon you but must also be felt by the masses within you, and that is why we encourage you all to read and gain a deeper understanding of such laws. Compassion cannot be bought or gained. It is inherent, held deep within your core, and as part of Creator, how could this not be so? Again, we encourage you to rediscover this compassionate side to your nature that for too long has been hidden under a bushel. We also wish to praise those of you working from a compassionate stance and ask that you continue your journey of exploration into this law.

Compassion is a gift from you to all sentient life, and, as previously discussed, is woven into the fabric of other laws. If we examine abundance we see that this requires compassion, as true abundance is not just material gains, but a deeper understanding of joy that incarnations can bring. This is demonstrated if we review the stories of the farmers and remember that the one that was joyous was able to manifest great gains on the earthly plane. We ask you to investigate others that have come before you and call your attention to Si Baba, Gandhi, Mother Theresa and other greats of your times. We ask you to review the compassion they emitted at a soul level and the teachings they brought to this planet. It is sufficient to say that compassion is entwined with all laws. We ask you to consider that all laws are interwoven, and as such it is all laws that lead back to the path of enlightenment.

The Universal Law of Retribution

This law is unlike any other discussed, and we draw your attention back to the fact that no action comes without a consequence, at a vibratory level or otherwise. So, it is on your actions we now contemplate and wish to remind you of the vibrational frequency that actions bear. We will now discuss another vignette to illustrate this point. There were two men who both wanted the same job. On the day of the interview man one, let's call him John, got up and knew he had prepared well for this day. He had studied hard and researched the company and believed he would get the job. Man two, David, took a blasé stance and felt superior and believed he would get the job. You may now be wondering about manifestation, and the key point is that all must marry up when manifesting your future plans. John had made an effort to prepare and taken action to be well informed, he had crossed all the Ts. He had also used the power of positive thought to encourage a favourable outcome, and it will not surprise you to hear that he was the successful applicant. This fable highlights that your actions, thoughts and beliefs count when in the manifestation process. Without the initial action there is no reaction. So, this law concerns striving; striving to do your best with the firm belief you cannot fail.

We draw your attention back to the keys of manifestation and how they clear the path for the manifestation process. Take heed that this also requires action on your part. We see your struggles on the earth plane, we bring the keys of manifestation to you now, but we remind you that without action on your part there can never be a reaction. Within the inner realms they fully understand this concept and we remind you of the tale of the old woman in her shoe. You need to cross all your Ts, as we said, and focus on what you truly wish for.

The Law of Retribution can also have adverse effects on the ability for you to reach enlightenment. Here, we discuss the ability to be able to forgive others and yourselves, as holding onto the past hurts does not serve you. More about this later, as we also introduce the key of forgiveness. Use this key as many times as necessary. This again brings us back to action and reaction, and we do not wish to go into great detail as you, the reader, fundamentally understands. It is within your reactions to perceived wrong doing to know where the truth really lies. This is to draw your attention back to the ability to 'turn the other cheek' and release deep rooted hurts for the good of the collective. This will greatly aid the ascension process of which we speak. We remind you again that this aids the grids on a planetary scale to clear. So, yet again your actions and reactions have a key role to play in the ascension process.

The Universal Law of Flux

This will be briefly touched upon, as all within the universe is in a state of flux. This law feeds into the Law of Creation in which we examined the ebb and flow. However, it differs in velocity as flux is seen as a mathematical equation and imparts that nothing is greater than the sum of its parts. That is to say that ebb and flow is a given constant, but the state of flux is much more about the velocity of the positive and negative vibrations which you find yourself in. This is seen throughout the cosmos and within the inner realms. The flux holds greater positivity than the negative vibrational patterning. Again, we remind you that to fully ascend, the flux within your space-time continuum must be of greater velocity towards the positive. This again brings up the importance of clearing negatively charged vibrations emitted from your stories, auras and DNA patterning. We have discussed many times how this feeds into the whole.

The Universal Law of Relations

This law concerns relationships. Again, all laws intertwine, but in this law we see relationships are continually in a state of flux. You may like a person one week and berate them the next. This again ties up with having free will to pick and choose your relationships. It has been discoursed that many have predetermined scripts with others planned before incarnation, due to lessons required in order to evolve to the light. However, now we request you look at your responses to less than satisfactory outcomes. We now mention the 'golden key of forgiveness' and encourage you to use this key as a gift to clear up old stories about actions perceivably done to you. Of this, many of you know of what we speak, as all on this plane are carrying old stories of injustices, done to you.

We now ask all of you to recall a story or a memory that makes you feel uptight, as it holds you back from becoming who you truly are. We do not wish to bring up uncomfortable feelings, but it is in this uncomfortableness you will see areas that require transformation. We will now examine an old story about a man and his wife. Their split was less than amicable, and both held on to negative patterning. The story of which we speak was seen three incarnations back, and now they find themselves married again, incarnated in the now. This present-day incarnation has affected their ability to live in a happy resonance, as they argue about monetary constraints, which in itself holds them back from harmonious interludes. If we go back three incarnations, we can see that the husband held the purse strings very tightly and allowed the wife no money of her own. All monies were counted out and put away for a 'rainy day', which incidentally never came. In the incarnation they now find themselves in, the roles were reversed, and the man had incarnated in female form. This money issue from three incarnations back is still playing out in the now. The couple often rowed about money, as the woman held on to the belief from three incarnations back that money is tight. The man, on the other hand, had learnt the lesson, being the downtrodden wife, and believed the couple should work together and support each other. So, on greater examination of the relationship, we can say to you that many of their issues had been created in the past. This is easily rectified if a new positive story is written for the pair, but here we see that relationships are complex. Compounded with this are the modern-day stresses which those of you in relationships find yourselves in. The clearing of this set of beliefs greatly aided the couple's relationship and they were able to move forward with a new resonance. This issue did not need to arise again during their next incarnations, and all was well.

You may now be pondering how it is possible to change roles, sex and why we incarnate again and again with the same set of souls, all playing out differing roles and stories. We say to you that during incarnations you will meet some souls again on your journeys, whilst others hold a new resonance. That is predetermined by you and you alone. The one true exception to this rule is that of twin flame relations. We bring this up now as there is much chatter of on your plane about this phenomenon. We say to you that it matters not what relationship you are in, but the lessons you learn from it. However, within the twin flame relations we see a continuation of journeying that can never cease. We say to you that it is equally as important in all relationships to clear negative patterning that may hold you back. So, we ask at this time that your concentration is placed upon any relationship in which you find yourself, regardless of the name you wish to give it. If a twin flame meets then there may be greater work to be done, as incarnation often follows incarnation, but that is not always the case. Some twin flames are together now at this time, as they have a contractual agreement to serve the masses. This is to be viewed without judgement, as those in a soul mate relationship have also made agreements about the lessons they need to learn and clear. In fact, their twin may be serving a higher purpose elsewhere in the cosmos, which has equally as great importance as those together today.

So, it is in your relationship with others we ask you to reflect. Reflect on the beliefs of the groups you find yourselves in. Do not judge those who have not started their journey of discovery, be ready and open to welcome them home to the light and remembrance of who they truly are. If you become detached from some souls during the course of your life, believe this is for the greatest good, as their journey is no less important than yours. Energetic resonance is partly accountable for such transitions in current times, as it is impervious to the tales you tell. That brings us back to the Law of Flux in which 'like attracts like', and so what may resonate one minute may not the next, as at a vibrational level one may feel a greater pull towards those that are in a more positive state of mind. This is why the message of this book is repeated many times, and it is the clearing of old beliefs we again emphasise. Souls change roles, sex and orientations during different embodiments, how could this not be so? If this was not so, great lessons would be lost, perspectives stagnated and growth impossible.

We now conclude the chapter that has taken us on a whistle tour stop of some of these laws of the cosmos. We remind you how such laws are intertwined and that if viewed in the totalitarian sense, you will miss out on key points of their make up. We again state these laws were made in order for the continuation of the cosmos, and we stress that due to upholding such laws life cycles become an infinite journey. A journey, for many, from the darker recesses into the light. Again, no judgement is cast upon this aspect of life as it maintains the momentum of infinity. However, such a concept leads us nicely onto the next chapter, in which we review the ascended masters, angelic beings of light and other such marvels.

Chapter 9

Ascension and the Ascended Masters,

Doctrines and the Way to the Light

We shall first discuss the ascended masters as all the beings that we discuss within this chapter and the next have, in some way, involvement with the keys. How is this possible, you may ask? It is possible as they aid the vibrational resonance during a key ceremony. We have not yet touched upon the ceremonies per se, and they will be discussed in much greater depth in the next chapters. It is important for you, the reader, to have an understanding of the beings of light, as they aid us greatly on the ascension journey.

The ascended masters; who are they, you may enquire? They have come to this planet before in many forms. You may know them under differing names but their message to your societies remained the same. We will now discuss a couple of these great beings of light.

Jeshua Ben Joseph

Jeshua incarnated on the earth plane in order to teach mankind the hidden truths about Source, universal Creator of all things. Many here now debate if this incarnation really occurred. We are here to say to you, yes, yes it did. He was sent from the inner realms to earth in order to teach you all one basic fact, and that is that you are all part of Source, the prime Creator. This, however, fell on deaf ears and over many millennia conflicts have arisen between different fractions and groups whom wish to place their own spin on this version of events. Jeshua tried many times to impart this fact during this incarnation. The people of this planet were not altogether ready to hear his tales. Jeshua found that some of his teachings were often stifled and worse, distorted.

Jeshua's life story was to show the people of this planet how to behave, what being in and of the light truly meant, and how this could be achieved. As we have seen throughout history at certain periods, advice from above has fallen on deaf ears. We acknowledge that the incarnation of Jeshua on the earth plane was at a time of many blocks around, within and upon your planet. Many of these blocks continue to be significant today. This incarnation occurred at this time on your planet as much unrest was felt, and this planet held great potential.

Each planet created is unique in its composition. If we take Saturn, for example, you will not find another planet that relies mainly on a hydrogen pressure quotient to remain on the axis it finds itself. That is to say, that the atmospheric pressure is of such velocity that at this time no sentient life is seen here. This planet was in orbit long before the creation of earth. It helps Source, Creator, in the formation of lay line structures that sit further away from the inner realms. Much of your solar system remains unexplored by yourselves, but we say to you that your solar system and planet are held in great esteem by the Creator. Creator made your world unique and one of the great creations upon your plane is that of object permanence and your ability to understand objects exist, even when they are not seen. Within many of the outer realm planets this phenomenon is not yet realised. Many of your discoveries are given to you as gifts. We discuss the theory of object permanence in order for you to deliberate the theories presented within this book and question existence as you know it. We ask you to consider the moon you see from your skies, and we ask you to ruminate the fact that although you may not always see the moon, you understand it is still there.

Why does this have relevance to the ascended master Jeshua Ben Joseph? It has much relevance, as we ask you to contemplate. Just because you have not seen this master with your eyes and observed him walking on the land, does that mean he does not exist? His core essence exists and continues to exist. We are not talking in the religious sense, as many teachings remain inaccurate such as the ability to walk on water and part the seas. If we whittle this down to the meaning these stories were intended to impart, we will see that creation was being discussed and that you, as Creator beings, are able to create great and momentous changes in your life, although we say to you wine did in fact turn to water. The tales that were imparted here were conveyed so that you, the human race, would question the power of your thoughts and beliefs. Jeshua incarnated from the inner realms where such anomalies are common place, as within these spheres many understand who they truly are, they trust and have belief in the fact that they hold the power for many miraculous events. The elders of these realms ensure the younger sentient life forms are taught this fact from an early age. Here, they are able to harness the power of their thoughts and we bring you back to the key fact that they understand energy and how to create at a vibrational level in the most glorious of ways.

Was Jeshua the son of Creator? We say to you, you are all the children of Creator. All life is Creator's child. You are all aspects of the God head and we write this book in the hope you may remember who you are. Jeshua did many miraculous things during the time of incarnation, and yes, he came back from the dead in his form, as life is eternal and that was the message from the Source. The message that you too are eternal children of God, and none of you are ever forgotten.

Jeshua showed you many things: how to heal through the power of thought, vibrations and action, how to provide for the masses, how to follow the Laws of the Universes, how to bring in the light. Jeshua remains in the esoteric realms and continues to present himself to you as a way of example. He was sent to this realm as a master and teacher of the light, the right and the realised self. That is to say, he knew who he was, Creator's son, without question. The question is did, or do, you? Did you and do you know who you truly are? Do you have this knowledge in the present day? Many do not, and we remind you again of the blocks that play out, the stories you tell and your actions and reactions that stop this realisation being truly known.

Jeshua continues to offer this support to all who seek his council. He imparts to you the time is nigh for great changes as earth ascends and he is only too happy to stand by your side should the need arise. He wishes you to know it is not by the doctrine he wishes to be known, but by the messages he brought to your world. He wishes to remind you that a path to the light is the objective and indoctrination of beliefs must cease. They hold you back from the greater understanding of the power of creation and Creator. He wishes to remind all of the great love of Source and the great rapture of love that Source holds for you all. It is the wish that you are reminded that you too are Creator beings, and again to inform you that there is no other way that this cannot be so. You see, all sentient life is created in the likeness of the Creator, whichever name you choose to give this supremacy of love light. Inner, outer realms – it matters not where you incarnate – all Creator's children are viewed in the same resplendent way by the supreme being known by many different names. Jeshua wishes to remind you that when you cry for help, no cry goes unheard. Many believe it does and has done throughout many incantations. We will now consider the rationale for this.

The rationale began many moons ago in times before William the Conqueror, before the Roman invasions to different lands, before the time of the good lord himself. We draw your attention, and digress slightly, to this phrase the good lord for a reason, as again much debate has been initiated by the phrase. What does this term truly impart? It imparts that there are 'good lords.' We, at this point, wish to remind you of the Laws of the Universes and discuss the Law of Creation: of ebb and flow, and the Law of Flux; vibrational energetic patternings held by sentient beings. If there are good lords, such laws state that there will be bad. We have previously determined that without this phenomenon all would cease to be.

We now wish to discuss the being you have named the devil. The devil exists in many forms and here we must question the belief about a fallen angel. Do you truly believe angels can fall from the grace of Source, or was this concept introduced to inform you that you have played out many differing roles on this plane you call earth? If all incarnations are to be believed and understood fully by your race, do you not see how you have played the role of the devil through many incarnations? It is worth pointing out that many souls upon Earth are unconscious of who they truly are. They still play out the role of the devil by living, acting and uttering unconscious thoughts, words and deeds. This has serious reprisal for others around them. Often, atrocious acts are carried out in the name of religion. We remind you that no such act comes from the light. By this, we will suggest you look at your actions and reactions. Are they of the light or do they have a lower vibrational pull? This cannot be rectified overnight, but we ask you to greatly consider the possibility that all of you within your incarnations on this plane have fallen from grace. If we whittle down this term, we will be able to observe the true construct of these words. That is to say, the fall from grace is the fall away from the love light, which many of you at this time are striving to reach and remember. So, we say on careful examination all have played the part of dark lords within your realm.

Back to the times before the good lord incarnated now, and as we resume this tale we wish for you to read the following text with an open mind. Your planet was created as an experiment to understand the outer realms of existence and was one of the first planets created further away from the light. Notice the word further, as there are now many realms further away from yours. Earth, Gaia, was one of the first, but there have been some before yours and we wish you to understand that not all planets created on the outer spheres have yet been able to return to the inner realms of existence. Ascension, as previously discussed, is a very complex process and the correct resonance must be in place before this can be achieved.

We now talk of previous times on your planet when this was attempted and look back on such times, as great learning came from these periods in your history. Of that we talk of times long forgotten by most sentient beings who reside on the planet today. These are the times of Lemuria and Atlantis. The ascension process was unable to occur as certain components were not understood and the elders were not congruent in their rhetoric, approach and mindset. They had mastered many concepts about their powers, but failed to work as a group collective, breaking into fractions. This allowed negative vibrations to, at points, clear too quickly, and in Lemuria we see the consequence as the downfall of a civilisation. This occurred as the collective vision had been lost and differing energetic tools, shall we say, were used by such fractions without considering consequences. When more of you on planet earth realise your powers, such misunderstandings cannot be allowed to happen again, as it took many, many millennia to reach the stages you now find yourselves in. We encourage you, the collective, to read the histories of these periods to enable you to understand about these periods in your evolution. Do not underestimate these times. Many may question if these periods in time, as you call it, in fact existed. We say to you they did. Again, we reinforce that this will not be allowed to be repeated as the importance of ascension to the higher realms of light cannot be underestimated.

We go back to your cries for help and whether or not they were heard by the supreme being of light. We say to you, your cries did not fall on deaf ears, as you are here in this ascension period for a reason. The collective spoke, and Creator listened, watched and waited for the perfect time.

Many of you began to question your beliefs, your reasons for being, shall we say. This was the plan since the time of creation itself, to have you question. You came many, many times to this planet in order to remember who you are. We say to you, all children are welcomed back to the love light, and so your cries were not forgotten.

We wish to remind you of the concept of time and the many countless centuries of suffering you have all experienced in one form or another. We say to you, in the most esoteric sense of the word, that time is not what you know it. Time was created by your kind to give a meaning to your experience, and when passing from embodiment to embodiment you could understand the journeys and experiences. You fully understood that time is a man-made concept when passing to the esoteric realms. That is why you were all so willing to go back and try again, and again. When you pass over, where do you think you go? You go, in fact, back to the love light, so you can review your journeys, lessons and accomplishments. Good and the bad, as you call it, are reviewed until they are understood in some way or another. When understood, you incarnate to do better and strive for a higher, greater, better way of existing in embodiment. This is true of any realm in which you incarnate and not strictly true of only one planet within the cosmos. We say to you, even in the inner realms there are different nuances that all strive to become. Again, we call your attention back to the Laws of the Universe, so you can understand without such endeavours all would cease to be.

The Great Buddha

Buddha incarnated some time before Jeshua. He again took on human form and his life purpose was to teach those whom he came into contact with the right way. That is to say, the way of enlightenment to the higher truths. His message was great in its simplicity and he came to show all mortals, the immortal life force they possessed. This had clearly been forgotten, hidden under a bushel, and he came to show the way to the light. Again, you will not be surprised to hear that he came from the inner realms of existence, and he knew his journey would, during this incarnation, be that of remembrance of his God self.

Buddha's philosophies included the greater understanding about harmonic resonance and if we whittle that down, we will see he understood at a vibratory level that all thoughts, actions and words hold a vibrational pull. This was deemed back then as karma, but today we wish you to understand that the Laws of the Universe remain the same. What he was discussing was that there is no action without reaction, no deed without consequence. He understood the vibrational essence of all things, he had a greater understanding of life force and creation. If we go back to the tale of 'the dog' when we reviewed the Law of Resonance, we impart that the Buddha understood that all Creator's beings, landscapes and land were part of the essence of love from the supreme being that is love. He understood vibrational rates, ebb and flow and flux, and about life within the denser plane of existence. Again, he tried to impart words of wisdom about how to live in the higher sense of the word. Again, for the main part, over many millennia this fell on deaf ears.

We use this term a lot within this book deaf ears and whenever it is used, it is done so to draw your attention back to the fact discussed at the beginning of this chapter, that your cries for help were heard by Creator. Again, we ask you to consider the facts. How many listened to the masters that walked these planes of existence? We ask you to consider the facts that within their teachings their messages had much in common, as have all great masters that have walked before. They understood the Universal Laws of Existence. They understood the power behind a thought, utterance and action. They came to show you an enlightened path. Again, some teachings were misconstrued, and the Buddha came to show all 'the path of least suffering.' The missing cog in the wheel, so to speak, is that within these teachings sentient beings forgot their creative powers and whilst the theories were correctly manifesting, you being creators was not fully realised.

We include these two masters within this book and that is not meant to negate other master's teachings. The reason they have been given particular reference is that of exempla. That is to say and request all readers consider other such teachings and the real messages they came to relay, of peace and love for all things, as all teachings lead back to the Source if you pardon the phrase. All teachings of the times held a vital message and that was this:

ALL THINGS ARE ONE, ALL PATHS BACK TO THE LIGHT REQUIRE SENTIENT BEINGS TO UNDERSTAND WHO THEY ARE. ALL MYSTERIES ARE LAID BEFORE YOU AND YOU HAVE ACCESS TO THEM ALL. ALL ANSWERS LAY WITHIN THE LAWS OF THE UNIVERSE. DOCRTINES ARE PRESENTED TO YOU AS GUIDES. MANY MESSAGES HAVE BEEN LOST DUE TO THE FIGHT BETWEEN WHAT IS DEEMED RIGHT. WITHOUT DARKNESS THERE CAN BE NO LIGHT. CONSIDER YOUR BELIEFS AND WE REMIND YOU OF THIS: THERE IS ONLY ONE TRUE WAY BACK TO ENLIGHTENMENT AND THAT IS TO CONSIDER WHO YOU ARE.

That concludes the chapter. We shall now continue the book by exploring the angelic realms and other beings of light.

Higher Self Key Set

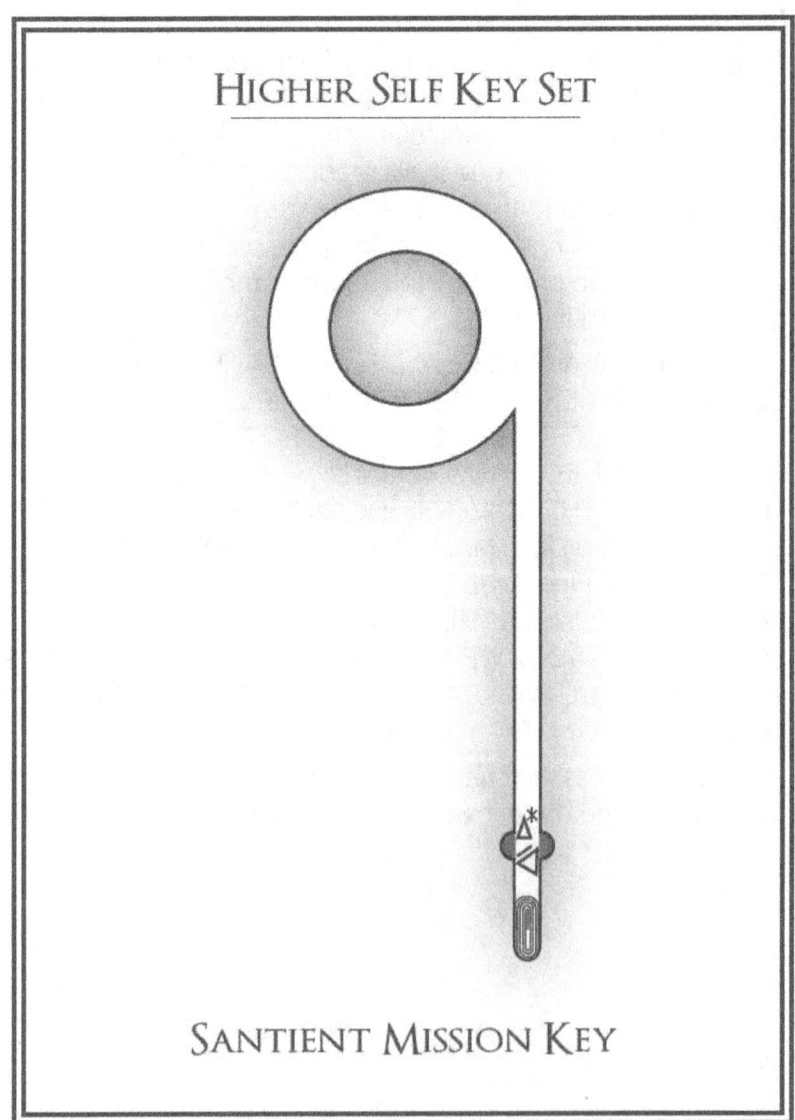

Santient Mission Key

Chapter 10

Angelic Realms and Other Such Marvels

The angelic realms have been around since the beginning. They are part of creation itself, that is to say they are creation and creators. Within the angelic realms there remains a hierarchy and it is possible, even here for angels, to work their way up the ladder, so to speak. Angels are a core part of creation and the saying, 'an angel sitting on your shoulder', is laughed about in the esoteric realms.

All sentient beings have such an angel but how many of you use them to their full advantage? None upon your planet and why is this? Is it because an angel has failed to be completely understood? Angels are the highest of high. They are the embodiment of Source. They have no fears as they are part of creation itself. They are the messenger and the message. They are truth personified. They are the light, of the light. They are beings of light; the most iridescent light you could ever see. They are the beauty in all things. They are so full of love of the essence of creation that sentient beings cannot fully understand their composition.

However, in recent years the angelic realms are heralding a comeback on your planet. Think about how your people can now connect to this realm. In the past we have seen these beautiful beings of light discussed but rarely felt. They have the ability to be here and there. They assist Source in many wonderful ways. They are the tick in the tock, the icing on the cake, the chocolate flake on your ice cream. They are at your beck and call and only too pleased to help. They can never leave you, just as you can never leave them. All sentient beings have an angel regardless of whether they are known to them or not. Within the inner realms, sentient beings know their angel by name. They work together, they understand that they are gifts from the Creator, just as angels know who they are as the gift. They hold no judgement, only the essence of love, and so when you ignore them or take them for granted they do not anger. They are truth, love and light personified.

The angelic realms assist greatly during some ceremonies. We shall now discuss the angels of light. It could be said that all angels are angels of light, but specific angelic beings have specific roles to play. The angels of light play specific roles, as when summoned and worked with they can access the dark areas to assist bringing in the light. When summoned they can be sent to the places that hold the shadows and clear stuck and stagnated energy. They have no fear and hold no fear as they were created this way to assist sentient life. During certain ceremonies they hold the space for negative energy to be transmuted by Source into a higher vibration of light. Such angels can be summoned if clearing planetary areas that are stuck in lower frequency vibrations. They are part of Source and creation, but they know who they are without question, as sentient life does not. They hold no lower vibrational patterning and as such cannot be swayed by the anguish felt by an incarnated soul. So, they are of the light and were created in the esoteric sense before sentient life. The angels of light are also commonly known as the 'Bringers of Light' as they project a beautiful harmonic resonance to all those they touch; all places they are called. We have included them in this text so those that are conscious of the angelic realms may beckon them more within this plane you call earth. They are currently not used to their full potential within your realm and we ask those of you reading this to call on them now. Take a moment to centre and ground and ask to be connected to The Bringers of Light. We discuss these angels first as they have not been as well known and appreciated on your plane of existence as the arch angels and other fractions have. We shall now continue to discuss the arch angels as they also play a highly important role at this time.

Arch angels; has anyone here really explored this term? Arch, when discussing these beautiful beings of light, is stated in reference to their arch-is-id-dual presence, not a word in totality, but an expression of the sum of their parts. If we break this down, we can assume greater understanding of their role within the space-time continuum. They act as an arch to all things. What are arches, one may cry?! They are the bridge to the divine presence, I am what I am. They are the doorway to higher truths, they are the love of Creator personified in the esoteric sense. If we now examine the word 'Id' within your vocabulary, we see it talks of your presence. The state of your presence devoid from altruistic motivations. It is the soul essence of Creator which resides in all of you. Within the term 'Id', we are not discussing soul stories genetically brought in, or the patterning of ancestral ties. Here, we discuss the pure essence of the presence all of sentient life holds and that is the core essence of Creator. No sentient life can be without this essence, as all came from Creator, even the dark lords.

If we examine the world dual, we understand there is duality in all things. Arch angels understand this concept in the highest sense of the word, and that is why they have no fear, as they have complete understanding about vibrational tugs and pulls, the ebb and flow, the flux and states of flux. They were created so that all sentient life can benefit from their council. They span spheres and realms, they are timeless, bodiless parts of creation. They show themselves to some in sentient terms and have been depicted as flesh and form. We say to you, it has been presented this way so you may know who they are. However, whether seen with second sight, or felt with vibrational resonance it matters not, as they are known truly by their essence.

We understand much has been written on certain arch angels and it is not the purpose of this book to recall all their individual attributes, as many texts have accomplished this.

We discuss them within this context to remind you to work with these supreme beings of light as they can offer your realm much assistance in the coming years. The arch angels assist with certain key ceremonies, due to their vibrational essence, and when a soul is moving timelines they can be very instrumental in assisting such shifts.

Back to their arch-is-id dual presence. We hope that you now have greater clarity on their role which is to enable sentient life to bridge the gap between their stories and the Id presence that all such souls hold, whilst understanding the duality of all things. They are not specifically supporting sentient life to forget the stories of their past, but to work with their Id presence and release the emotional response that has kept them stuck in duality of existence. Let us explore this. We understand all will cease without this dual aspect of creation. Again, we make it clear that it is the resonance with this duality that makes a planet and its life form remain in lower vibrational spheres, the outer realms, further from the light. So, in conclusion, arch angels are worth much pontification when deliberating their attributes and they are only too happy to assist you to know them better.

There are many, many more angelic fractions but the last fraction we wish to discuss is that of the seraphim. These beautiful beings of light may be represented as golden angelic beings. We will now explore their history and their inclusion in the ascension story and the keys. Such angelic beings are the 'oldest of old' and they were created to hang out with Source. These angelic beings help sentient beings in many ways, and they can be called upon to aid individual trauma and traumatic episodes and such incidences within and upon your realm. Within the inner realms they are known by their presence and in the esoteric sense they are creators of peace. They are brimming over with the sense of love light and they hold great magnitude of such love for all sentient life. They overflow with joy and when you call them in they can transmit a great sense of peace to your very being. We ask you now to take a moment, to call in these amazing beings of light, as they wish to make their presence known on this plane at this time. Again, they may aid you out of the shadowy recesses that reverberate through your soul due to the old stories that have kept you stuck for so many millennia. They work with Source in certain ceremonies to aid traumatic shifts, they hold the space for such traumas to be sent to Creator's light, whilst beaming down the love light held at their very core.

We now take a moment to consider the angelic realms and remind you how you see them through every doctrine which studies esoteric beliefs. They have not excluded one of your books that you study on your plane. Just as this book is presented to include all fractions of religious connotations, we ask you now to unite on the fact that not one of your doctrines has excluded their presence. How have they survived in all their forms throughout the millennia? They have survived as they are part of the essence of creation. The essence of love light, the essence of hope and messengers for the divine.

We shall now review the other such marvels, and in this we include the angelic being you have come to know as Metatron. Metatron joins some ceremonies as he enables you to understand the ascension path and your clarion call; that is your call back to service. He has been working closely with Melchizedek to oversee the ascension process and with this we draw special attention to inner and outer planetary grids. Metatron has been overseeing the alignment of such grids and structures. Metatron is a giant in angelic terms, as his expanse holds no bounds. By that we come to understand that Metatron works with a planet and its people during ascension and the shaking up of lower vibrational structures. Metatron holds a powerful angelic presence and understands the formations of geometric grids and such systems that lead us back to Source, the power of one. He holds council with others in the esoteric realms, and we can be assured his help is called upon when deliberating mathematical and binary combinations that are required to maintain the status quo at a vibrational level. This is too complex for the human mind at this time, but those working within the mathematical fields should call on him for direction as he is only too pleased to assist in such matters.

Metatron can be described as a powerhouse if we look at the resonance of energy his being evokes. He works closely with some souls, in many differing realms of existence, to bring about fundamental changes in geometric patterning and codings that aid planetary infrastructures. Those reading this with an interest in geometry should again call upon his esoteric powerful mind. We say the word mind to you, so you may understand, but the angelic mind is free from the constraints of sentient life forms. Metatron will be aiding some souls greatly in the future by giving them a cosmic understanding of geometric patterning and the resonance this brings forth. We remind you that Source created such presence to greatly assist sentient life and without such great beings of light much of the ebb and flow would be lost. Life would diminish, as it is the likes of Metatron that enable geometric structures such as grids to remain in a state of mutability, without the loss or pull towards the states of lower vibrational patterning.

Lord Maitreya works closely with the keys and The Key Keepers. He often makes an appearance in the sacred ceremonies of the keys as he is a great teacher for all sentient life. Again, in the esoteric sense he is not seen in embodiment but is embodiment. This phrase can be broken down, as if we consider the term embodiment we notice that embodiment may be taken literally to mean 'of in body', or, in the higher sense of the word, to mean in oneness of all things. The message Lord Maitreya wishes to impart through this text is the power of one. The power of one fleeting thought can change a life as thoughts are the most important thing you own. He joins in ceremonies to oversee that all stories are cleared, and he holds the sacred space for teachings that are required to move forward in harmonic resonance.

In certain ceremonies, elemental realms may make an appearance. We mention them as they work with certain sentient beings within this realm of realms to aid specific evolutionary structures. By this we mean the land, vegetation, animal and tree life. There are those of you reading this that may feel a certain calling, shall we say, to work with the nature and eco-systems on your plane. We asked you to be open minded about the elemental fractions as do you truly believe that there cannot be existence within existence. We draw your attention back to old texts such as that of Greek mythology and fairy tales. Inner realm spheres understand such beings of creation, and all work as one for the good of all.

Much of this text may feel impossible to comprehend to some reading this book. We draw your attention back to times in your history. Do you understand that at one time in evolution 'you all' perceived the world as flat? There was a time when you thought that if you walked too far, you could fall off the edge of the world. How we laughed in the esoteric sense, not at you, dear ones, but at your innocence and perceptions in the ability you perceived as creation. The insular beliefs you held, the inability to grasp the vast expanse of creation. This was to be so, as you needed to learn about the beauty you beheld around you. It is through lessons such as this you can truly step into your sovereignty of whom you truly are.

We illustrate this point to open your mind to differing possibilities. Possibilities that have remained hidden for thousands and thousands of years. This was, in fact, so history, as we knew it, did not repeat itself. We could not have a repeat of earlier times upon your planet, when all was lost through unconscious acts. Here, we are talking once again of Atlantian and Lemerian times. So, you regressed back into infancy and you started again, learning about vibrational resonance, until you came to a place that you find yourselves now. The Mayans, whose calendar ended at 11:11 December 2012, did not predict the date for the end of the world, but the new beginning. The beginning of a new enlightened period in your history as your planet ascends back to the light of creation.

The ascension process is fully underway, regardless of your consciousness about this fact. However, we say to you that the unconscious will awaken from their slumber, as more and more facts and truths are revealed. We ask you, the conscious, to steer them on their journey without condemnation or pity, but with love and acceptance for their own unique resonance. There are those that may leave this realm, but they are never forgotten as eternity is indisputable, irrespective of whether it is understood as a concept or not.

We draw your attention back to the Laws of the Universes and ask you to contemplate this. Has your world ever ceased to exist throughout history and destructive patternings and actions by your kind? We say to you no, it has not. Historians can clarify this. Look back to the ice age, the iron age and the debated planetary life of what was Atlantis and Lemuria. It has never ceased, just as you cannot cease, you are part of creation. Sentient life changes shape and form, but it is endless in its ability to be. Some mysteries of life are now being presented to you, so you may examine the facts. If you pontificate or examine this with an open mind it matters not. Facts remain facts, laws remain laws, virtues remain virtues, life remains life. The great expanse of life remains a mystery to many. We ask you to take what you will from these texts, question, deliberate and pontificate. However, at the end of the day when you turn out the lights, we hope this text has stirred some deep cellular memories, and that is the quest.

Chapter 11

The Esoteric Realms and The War of the Worlds

The War of the Worlds is included within these teachings as it has great relevance to some of your history and the governmental structures you see today. Worlds were not always in the status quo you see them in today. By status quo, we refer to the locking down of interplanetary grid systems. We saw in the early years of planetary creation much upheaval in certain planets in the outer spheres. We have discussed your universe and world were amongst the first to be created within the outer realms and that this experiment occurred as the inner realms required some vibrational resistance to remain in orbit to maintain life. This was established by trial and error, although we also convey to you that there can be no error in creation. By that we inform you once again that as soon as a planet, soul or sentient life is created, Creator's great love for all creation cannot be underestimated. Even though mistakes were made, sentient beings' journeys continued esoterically and often they found themselves incarnating within a different realm, as free will stipulates.

The esoteric realms cannot be understood fully by sentient life form no matter where you incarnate. They are a completely different realm of existence, although they follow the same etheric rules of the universes which you go by. They are influenced by sentient life and its struggles and triumphs. The esoteric realms grow in structure in line with all creative processes, planets and life. Source is the realm of all of creation, esoteric or otherwise. This cannot be placed into words but it can, however, be felt, believed and known. For some this is not enough.

We wish to take you back further in the history of creation to a time no sentient being can contemplate, a time that time forgot, as there was no time and this construct will be deliberated within the following chapters. There was just simply energetic resonance devoid of thought and structure. Imagine, if you will, an empty plane of existence where all is vibrating at the same time, no deviance in resonance other than that of purity. Now, imagine many such energetic planes merging into a mass of one resonance of purity and love. Here, we are noting the resonance of the vibration, that of purity where light reaches matter and harmonic patternings emit frequencies. The first frequency omitted is that of Om. Om is the crux to all life and if you study the law of relativity much sense can be made of this concept. Within this aspect of creation, we then see this vast expanse of resonating matter meeting its polarised opposite, anti-matter, and a fraction is produced. This in turn sparks a reaction and refractory resonance in which matter can grow. The growth of positive matter and cellular structures within this vibrational refractory period is possible if the correct cellular structures and materials for cell growth are in play. So, we see a single cell that then attracts its similar structural resonance and, if conditions are correct, we see further cells being produced. All such cells have one thing in common, that of the powerhouse. The powerhouse of a cell is the mitochondria. It acts as an energetic centre and hub to ensure life continues. So, the beginning of creation could in fact have stemmed from a singular cell.

We now ponder where the energetic resonance devoid from thought materialised. We ask you to go beyond matter and anti-matter to the esoteric realms. We say to you that all of creation and energetic vibrations stem from here, as Source is the Source of all things. To try to explain this concept further would be futile as it is much beyond the conceptual understandings of the human mind. We shall say this, that you have only just touched the surface in understanding energetic resonance and its power. We again compel those working within these complex fields to utilise the esoteric realms when exploring such concepts. We include this information in this chapter to inform you that creation was no accident, it was, however, a grand experiment by the super power, the Creator, to be able to create vast and marvellous things, beings, life and structures that expanded esoteric knowledge. We will bring you back to the concept of ebb and flow and relay to you that such creations were necessary in order to maintain the essence of love. If we break this down further, love cannot exist without love. Of this we speak of the resonance and vibrational patterning of the essence, which goes beyond words and again conceptualisation. We now discuss lower frequency and energetic resonance. Again, we ask you to open your minds to the profound thought that lower frequency resonance is produced from love as all energetic patterning contains the vibrational frequency of Om in differing states. What is this resounding vibration if not the essence of love? Om is the essence of creation and the created in its differing states.

Enough of this, as we fly back to the beginning of this chapter and The War of the Worlds. Planets within the inner and outer realms had been created to allow incarnated life to continue to exist, and we include your realm within this ethology. It is the study of behaviours we now seek to discuss. Many moons ago, before much sentient life had incarnated within the outer spheres, the outer realms had no concept of how precious life was and so within the outer universes wars, terror and destruction was common. A certain planet had come under very dark rule and the dictatorship of this realm spread far and wide. The sentient life was not deemed as precious and an eye for an eye was considered acceptable behaviour.

We mention this phrase 'an eye for an eye' in the hope that this term can be reviewed by you, the people of earth. This term has been floating around too long, and within the inner realms of existence do you really believe that they revenge those that have been perceived as doing another wrong? We tell you categorically not. Many battles on your planet have been, and are being, fought due to this philosophy. This is found within many of your countries, governmental structures and filters down into your corporations, your homes and your personal relationships.

We continue with the story of old, in saying that such was this dictator's lack of understanding about the world in which he lived, he believed he owned it. The audacity of this presumption was taken seriously in the esoteric spheres and inner realms, and it was felt that this danger may spread to neighbouring realms, as this species had much advanced technology. We have mentioned before that many sentient beings may be much further advanced in their ability to understand matter, sound waves, resonance and mathematical calculations, and all these attributes together make time and space travel a realistic possibility. We divulge that this had indeed become possible within the realm we shall name Orion. Within this realm fear ruled and travel to other realms was near completion. Source decided that this could not be allowed to continue as this spread of destruction would affect other created spheres. We bring you back to the salient point of free will, and we wish you to know that due to this universal and esoteric law, much of the chaos and carnage could not be altered. However, due to this exact law there were fractions upon this realm that broke free of the tyranny, regime and repressive rule and unlike the masses, were able to connect to higher guides, esoteric realms and the light. This became the saving grace upon the planet, although many lost their embodiment in the process. Such tyrannical rule always loses the fight no matter how many millennia pass, as the pull towards love holds greater resonance over lower vibrational energies. These fractions broke free and fought back, and we remind you again of the fact that thoughts are the most important thing you own, and it was through the power of collective consciousness that many of the autocratic structures break down. We are not talking here of the ascension process per se, but the ascension of the thought process to that of light.

Across the planet many souls opted out of this dictatorship. Due to the dwindling followship, this dictator upped the game. He ordered many to be rounded up and many disappeared from the planet. However, amongst the fractions a new ruler had emerged, a ruler sent by Source to aid this land. An incarnated soul with knowledge from far away lands that had the ability to reawaken masses to whom they truly were. The dictator at this time had become an old man, and his offspring did not hold the same resonance as they had been totally spoilt by the reality in which they lived. They believed they were not expendable you see, as these beliefs had been installed in them from an early age. We are not saying there was not sentient life lost in the battles that ensued. We are making the point that this war was not fought to gain revenge, light against dark. It was fought as souls under the dictatorship had lost their free will, a universal right for all, due to the oppressive regimes, mind control, tyranny and corruption. We remind you to review the societal norms in which you find yourselves as free will is a law. It is a law that cannot be breached, and we say to you that those that do so will face retribution, not out of revenge and an 'eye for an eye', but from love.

We see in the end of this tyrannous tale, that the oppressive, repressive structures broke down and although some repression remained, it was in a diluted form. We remind you here of the choices you make during the ascension process and impart that such tyrannical regimes will not survive the ascension process as they have continued here on this planet for too many millennia. Source has spoken and wishes for all to be informed that destructive plots will be taken down, lands will belong to the masses and not the few. Powers will return to the collective for the highest good. Whilst many reading this will say this is not possible in our lifetimes, Creator has decreed that this will be so, as the evolutionary route you have all been travelling down will cease, and new timelines will be forced into play. By force we do not mean that in the way it may be read, we mean that enough of your kind has spoken, there are mass awakenings that will continue over the next few generations. Free will of your kind will reign supreme, and the love light will return to planet earth. We say to you; what can you do to aid this process? We say to you, work with Source, Creator, and follow your hearts. Stand up for what you believe in and send out positive vibrations to the universe.

We now bring you back to the story of the Keeper of the Keys and say to you, it matters not which way you choose to clear old stories. Instead, it matters that you clear them nevertheless, as they hold you back into stepping into a new vibrational resonance. We shall continue the next chapter by examining the sacred ceremonies and the keys.

Chapter 12

The Sacred Ceremonies and The Keys

The keys have many uses and we have discussed that they are held within vaults within the Akashic records. We have also determined that the keys have not been in use on your planet for many millennia, as they hold a high resonance that would not have been sustainable with the energies upon your planet. By this we mean that sentient life would not have coped with the powers held within the keys, and many would have presumed and believed that this was magic.

With many souls now awake and awakening to many possibilities, Source felt the time was right for these healing gifts to be reintroduced. This took some careful planning, and this began long before some incarnated on this plane, in order for the message of the keys to be safely resumed in this realm. It was important that those bringing the message of the keys had encountered many human experiences in order to prepare them for the reintroduction. There was to be no repeat of earlier times within the cosmos, when much sentient life was lost due to inexperience. Such mistakes could not be allowed again.

Many planets have the use of such keys. However, many do not. The rationale behind this is down to the energies of the planet, the life force and the beings. Certain structures are required for the keys to be used in a safe and respectful manner and in this we include interplanetary and outer planetary grid structures. That is to say, there must be clearer grids around a planet before the energetic resonance of the keys can be introduced from the esoteric sense. This will be explained in greater depth in the next chapter, but now we shall begin to explore the sacred ceremonies of the keys.

We begin by noting that all keys at this time on the planet must be given by the Lord and Master, Melchizedek. Not all planets have to go through this process, but on reintroduction it is deemed as highly important that the keys are reintroduced in this way. We have already examined a time when this was not done within this book and take you back to the planet called Astonia where during the ascension process many perished in floods due to incorrect use of the keys. On other planets that have ascended back towards the light, The Key Keepers, and note we have plural here as there are many trained in this art, are able to call on certain keys to aid sentient beings clear old stories and restore hope. This will be reintroduced on earth when the time is right, but for now reintroduce it back through Melchizedek and the Keeper of the Keys, whom has had specialist training in the esoteric sense on the reintroduction of this ancient art.

The ceremonies are given only if the sentient receiving the key is ready for the energetic restructuring, patterning and the new harmonic resonance. The energies experienced within a ceremony come directly from Source and the sacred space is held by Melchizedek and other beings of light. When fully integrated back into a realm, the ceremonies are then overseen by the key keeper, however other beings of light may still join the sacred event, such as the angelic realms, masters and teachers appropriate for the sentient whom is in receipt. All ceremonies are adapted to the sentient who is receiving the keys as Source knows which stories, energies and restructurings are required for that soul's journey to progress in the highest ways.

Source is the energy behind the transformations that occur within the sentient energy field, and this is why such powerful transformative occurrences may transpire. We have discussed that the keys were founded by Source in order

The Sacred Ceremonies and The Keys

that no planet's information and structures were lost and so that grid systems were carefully monitored and there was a catalogue of sentient beings' structures within certain realms. When we whittle down such structures, we note that genetic encodements, DNA patterning and cellular structures are held within certain keys. Within other keys that remain in use in the outer spheres, we see keys that aid emotional patterning and responses in operation. They are used as long as the sentient has raised their energy field to a certain level and may be utilised to clear trauma, darker energies, anxieties, fears, depressive thoughts and genetic patterns. Within these specific ceremonies the Akashic records are accessed and old stories are thrown out at high speed, and a new higher perspective pattern is gifted to the recipient.

We now examine such a ceremony in greater depth as the use of such keys are important in the ascension process. There is a set of keys used for emotions that clear patterns and lift a being into a new resonance. By this we discuss how the aura is cleansed, the old energies are released as stories are discarded and thought processes are changed, so that reactions to events are not triggered in the same way. We have discussed that many beliefs and stories have come from many blocks experienced through many incarnations, both here and within other realms. Such stories hold back the species from realisation of whom they truly are, cause disease and, as previously determined, keep sentient beings in negative patterning. Within the set of keys that can be utilised we see keys that unlock such patterning and in this we include keys that aid not only depressive states, but individual keys that address such issues as jealousy, forgiveness, deceit, awareness of higher self, greed, destructive patterning and trauma states. By this we define trauma states to be an energetic resonance with trauma states, drama, gossip and misdeeds. Let's look at some more examples of which we speak.

We shall first take a look at the key that aids the restructuring of traumatic states and ask you to consider what is trauma? Trauma states can be experienced in many ways; through sight, smell, touch, hearing and differing scenarios. To make it traumatic, and have a remembrance that is less than optimal, most of a sentient being's senses have been employed as a first point of reference. So, when one finds themselves in a less than optimal situation, let us take an explosion as way of example, the first sense that is utilised is the hearing. The blast if you like, triggers a chemical reaction in the brain, the fight or flight process that installs a certain amount of fear. The next reference point that may be provoked is that of sight, smell and maybe skin and sensory perceptions due to heat, depending on how near the explosion one is. Now, if we take the first sense of hearing and whittle this down as way of example, it is the loud sound of the bang that is the furthest away from the vibrational resonance of the sound frequency we see displayed in the sound of Om. We have discussed this sound of creation before, and we bring up such comparisons in order to highlight again, vibrational structures of lower and higher vibrational tones, sounds and noise, in order for you to understand their effects.

Back to the explosion that is sensed in many ways. Now we wish you to consider that it was not a pleasant experience to be involved in such an event, and the next time the sentient hears a big bang they immediately associate such a noise with this traumatic event. This in turn triggers chemical reactions in the brain to a greater or lesser extent dependent on the individual. Now let us consider there are many incarnations where such trauma may be running with this individual. Let's say in ten incarnations back they incarnated near a volcanic eruption, they are more likely to experience a greater reaction to the explosion than the next person whose experience of such events are not nearly as traumatic. Compounded with this we also take on other's resonance as their actions and reactions to such an event, due to a cause and effect, are stored in the memory cells.

Now we see certain deep rooted cellular memories come into play, and such memories are stored in the subconscious areas of the brain, such as within the amygdala. Promptly, this traumatic event, due to the feelings it evoked, may start to filter into other areas of a sentient being's life force, and by that we mean interruption of positive patterning within this brain sphere. This causes certain areas to become devoid of light and blockages may be seen in the auric field and the body. When we examine this further, we see the person involved with such a trauma develops a knee problem and goes on to have much reconstructive surgery. If we link this back to the amygdala and observe electrical activity, we will see an unhealthy electrical impulse within this region that may be miniscule. It may not be picked up by current systems seen within your realm that monitor such diminutive vibrational patterning. However, it has been a causal reason for the sentient in question to have resistance in moving forward. This is just one example of many. However, it is important to note that cellular memories are held within an energy field of individuals and this has not really been explored in depth within your realm. However, if such traumas are healed and transmuted by accessing the esoteric realms, we see a new resonance of energy come into play. So, the sentient being who had the traumatic experience is no longer running the old scripts that caused the blockages and is able to walk forward without this story reverberating in their field. What does this mean for this being? Well, it means that they remember the lessons they gained from such trauma, let us say how to help others in that moment. Working as one group consciousness, regardless of creed, race, sexual orientation and demographic background for the good of all, they have now rid themselves of the energetic vibration of fear that froze them at a point in time, so they kept reverberating this traumatic situation. They are then free to move forward in their life with a new spring in their step. Here, the fear of experiencing life, to a certain extent, has been transmuted and in its place the sentient is able to move forward without this fear running alongside them.

We shall now examine a further scenario that which includes drama and gossip. This key is included in the group of keys that we have named trauma states, as drama and gossip cause sentient life to experience shocks in their energy field. We shall discuss an extreme example of such shocks as a way of reference.

It should be noted, however, that even less extreme examples of gossip and dramas cause some interruption within a sentient being's field, for example, the gossip you may be exposed to when discussing a family member or neighbour down the road. You may hear of a drama taking place where a couple has rowed, or drama was caused over a death due to family squabbles about the estate. These less acute examples have been highlighted to make you ponder on such utterances and stories that play out in your normal daily lives. Such gossip and dramas would not hold the same resonance if cleared from the energy field and they would become just that, a story. As a result, responses to such events would dramatically change. With the change in response, such events lose their significance and so with many changing their response to such events the story is able to become transmuted to what the sentient hearing the story can do to help. What we are saying here is that when old stories lose their dramatic pull, reactions change to a higher vibrational state. That state where gossip is not spread, and beings are able to help others get over such events in a faster less destructive way. Let us now examine the repercussions of a dramatic event.

Mrs Smith three doors down has a nasty accident and her husband walks out on her as he feels he cannot cope with the demands this has made on his life. The news spreads to the street in which she lives, and people begin to gossip. "Oh, how terrible," they exclaim, "we always knew her husband was a cad and a rotter." The story becomes embellished and instead of the husband walking out because he could not cope with the situation in which he found himself, the story is twisted and rumours of an affair spread. Speculation as to the person who he left her for begins, and soon we have a whole new drama being portrayed. The poor man and his wife become whispers behind hands, and no one actually calls on the wife in the street to see how she is, leaving Mrs Smith isolated and feeling unloved.

Meanwhile, the news of the affair twists and turns as these things do, until Mr Smith is having an affair with the woman who works in the local shop. She is also married, and the news gets back to her husband. The rest is history, as we now see two broken marriages with no substantial cause. The only cause being that Mr Smith panicked when faced with a traumatic event in his life. Had one or two of the neighbours cleared the resonance of drama and gossip, we may see a significantly different outcome. The neighbours who held higher vibrational patterning stopped the stories dead and gave greater resonance to how Mrs Smith was coping. Soon, many of those in the street were calling on Mrs Smith to enquire how she was. They supported her through this incident and Mrs Smith was able to feel their support. Meanwhile, the gossip and slander had been halted and Mr Smith met some locals in his favourite watering hole. They got talking and suggestions of where Mr Smith may find support for this trauma in the local vicinity began. Now the whole story changed resonance and the rest is history. Two marriages were saved as some of the neighbours had changed their energy about gossip and drama.

The third key in the set we name 'trauma states' is that of misdeeds. If you remember a time you felt that someone had wronged you, it will possibly bring up a feeling or emotion that is still playing out in your energy field. If we take the previous scenario as way of a vignette, we can see in the first instance that Mr Smith has been aggrieved by a misdeed, the rumour of the affair. We now look at how he handled the first scenario and we say to you, he wanted revenge. He never liked Mr Jones from number seven, and decided it was him and his wife who had started such rumours. He was hell bent on revenge, even though Mr Jones was not involved in this story. He was always busy with work, and often very tired when he got home. This made him somewhat aloof and judgements were made on this, causing Mr Jones to be discussed as a person who 'thought he was above everyone else.' Do you see where this is going? Mr Jones had been on the receiving end of gossip which now started a whole new story and Mr Smith decided, after a drunken debacle, to assault Mr Jones on his way home from a very long day. Mr. Jones had then experienced a trauma state and began having extreme panic attacks as, unknown to Mr Smith, Mr Jones had been beaten frequently in childhood. Mr Jones alas lost his job, and his marriage crumbled due to his mental state, and the rest is history, as they say. We now see three failed marriages and disrupted lives due to idle gossip and drama.

We make a point of this story to highlight the reverberations of one small act of tittle tattle! Some may now be saying that this outcome may be due to lessons each sentient being has come to learn from differing experiences. We say to you that whilst this may be so, for the planet to truly ascend such dramas need to cease. We have discussed how it may take many incarnations for a soul to learn the lessons on this plane of existence, and the lessons to be fully realised. So, we bring back the key ceremonies now, so a way is forged so that such stories do not play out for generations to come. We again highlight that there are many ways of resolving such issues, and it is the outcome we wish to be specific about. The key ceremonies do, however, clear many old stories and the vibrations of such that are held within your species' energy fields, and Source wishes to gift those in receipt of these ceremonies with a new energetic resonance. This clears a path for such traumatic events not to be played out within your realm and your lives. We have already discussed how this feeds into group consciousness and the grids, bringing the planet back into the light at greater speeds.

Within the key ceremonies the aspect of self that is worked upon is that of the higher self. We shall discuss this in detail within the next chapter. The higher self is the aspect of self that connects to Creator, and this higher body of self can have many blocks. We shall now discuss some of the esoteric realms, the keys and the higher self.

Judgment Key Set

Integrity Key

Chapter 13

The Esoteric Realms, The Keys and The Higher Self

We shall commence this chapter by having an overview of the esoteric realms of existence. There are many aspects of this realm that will not be included within this text. However, during ascension much more information will become available to you as a species. We shall start by saying that the God head is supreme, and, as previously established, is the Creator of all things. We say this to you, so you may not become confused when discussing the esoteric realms and feel that they are not overseen by Source, as these realms are indeed overseen by the supreme being of love light. We discuss esoteric realms in the plural sense, as we see realms within realms, much like we see within creation of the planetary structures. By this we mean the universes, inner realms and outer spheres.

Within the esoteric spheres there remain outer fringes that souls may access when passing from incarnation to incarnation. Here, we are discussing the realm of the stuck soul. You may have experienced this as a ghostly projection, and there has been much debate about this upon your planet. There are many sceptics that do not believe in the paranormal experiences some have encountered. We say to you that this is because they have shut down this area of recognition as they do not wish to perceive there is an afterlife. They have not come to accept the infinite state of creation and have not opened up to the possibility of many incarnations. In due time this will cease, as many more experience the fact that an afterlife before embodiment exists. We draw your attention to many that have passed and seen the light and returned to the plane of embodiment, and this is seen as a gift to your planet, so the word may spread about their experiences.

The term seen the light has been mentioned as it is often quoted within your realm and we ask you to consider its true meaning. What is seeing the light? We say to you it is the reawakening from the slumber, the grasping of a different perception of belief. Many within the outer spheres are travelling such journeys so they can reawaken to whom they truly are. We remind you again of the darker fractions of society and categorically state that this occurs for a reason. Not to draw out this point, it is placed within this text at this point to discuss judgement of others. This will be debated with much gusto during the next chapter. Back to the outer fringes, esoterically speaking.

Many souls within the outer sphere planets having forgotten who they are and feel a certain resonance with a place and time. If we take the headless coachman that has been mentioned in many of your ghostly books, as many have heard a headless tale or two, we, in the esoteric spheres, understand that an un-awakened soul may become trapped. They have passed from embodiment but feel a certain vibratory resonance with a place and time. We discuss the fact that they are not conscious of who they are, and most souls that return to a realm have not fully crossed to the esoteric spheres in entirety. By this we inform you that such beings rarely do harm, and they often left embodiment in less than ideal circumstances. Other rationales for a soul becoming stuck in the outer esoteric spheres remain somewhat the same, however, they may remain in the outer esoteric spheres as they are attached to other souls. The thing that all souls who are held within this outer esoteric realm have in common is that they lack the understanding of who they truly are. That is to say, they are not clear about the state of infinity, and this infinite ability to move from incarnation to incarnation. This is not realised.

We draw your attention back to the time when you all believed the earth was flat and use this analogy once again to highlight that you didn't know what you didn't know. We say that some souls in the outer esoteric realms become stuck due to this very fact. We include this in the explanation of the esoteric spheres as some reading this will be able to help them across. Others reading this will skip through this text, feeling this does not apply to them. No judgement is made on this however you may be right. Those reading this text may be drawn to the performing arts, the sciences, the nurturing of the young, the teachers, the agriculturalists, or metrological studies, to give some examples. For the planet to ascend it has some relevance, as trapped souls cause some interruptions in light due to their vibratory rate. This can be described as soul vibrations, and those held within the outer esoteric realm have many of the same issues they incarnated with. They have not had a life review and discussed their next journey, as it is in the passing to the esoteric realm, light is shed on the journey and a remembrance is initiated to who you are. The moving of such souls from the outer esoteric areas back to the light is important, as a soul may be trapped in a spot for many millennia. For those reading this text that have the ability to aid souls in such a way, please take a moment to do so.

Within the esoteric realms we also find that those souls returning from incarnation having a settling in period back to the light, and as Creator beings are able to create a remembrance of life in embodiment with none of the hardships they encountered. Some souls on the journey of remembrance following an incarnation may become stuck in the settling in period (we include those souls that have travelled darker routes). This mainly applies, once again, to the outer realms due to the lack of understanding of whom they truly are. We use this term a lot within this text, as it is relevant to all outer sphere planets and incarnations; this journey is back to remembrance. We have stated that this remembrance may, in fact, take lots of incarnations to complete. We draw your attention to the fact there is no time in spirit, or within any plane of existence come to that. Within the inner realms they understand this concept and judge the passing of the incarnated experience as skills to aid the soul to grow.

You may now be querying how the Akashic records are held in a space-time continuum, as mentioned at the start of this book. We say to you the word continuum has much relevance and the space in time of which we talk is simply that of experience. We use the word time loosely, so you may understand the concept of the great living library and the place the keys are stored. Within the inner realms this is simply known as the library of catalogues held within the esoteric mind of many minds of Source. Although the language differs from planet to planet, they have a much greater understanding of this vast expanse of esoteric knowledge. We bring you such facts now so that you may start to muse over your perceptions of reality. We shall now digress slightly from the task of explanation to discuss perception of reality.

This section may blow your mind. Please read with your mind open to many possibilities. We start by stating 'there are possibilities within possibilities.' If we scrutinise such a concept we see many possible realities in which you may be living. That is to say, if there is no time, all time is happening now, within this moment, and therefore time becomes a social construct. That is why there has been much written on this concept of living in the moment of now. You use various tools to aid this visionary reality that the only moment is now. We encourage you all to carry on contemplating this expression and use such tools as mindfulness in your daily structure to remind yourselves of this fact. You may ask if the concept of time is man-made, and as such are all incarnational experiences happening at once? Creator states they are, and they are not. To truly understand this would take a million years but if we said to you time waits for no man, what would be your initial response?

We digress but we wish you to consider that time is a construct for planet earth, to keep you excited about the creations you are yet to experience. Those that can see no future, just bleak apathy, will find that time slows down. Many outer sphere realms have the feeling that a day, as you know it, is very, very long. Much exploratory physicists have begun to write on the quantum aspect of time. We say to them, refine this research and as a way of a pointer, look at refractory periods between two subatomic structures. Refractory periods have not been explored in great depth within your realm and have been related to subatomic monocular structures. It is the refractory period of which we speak, and although this has a complex equational variance, we ask you to study this further. Continuing further into the concept of time, we ask you to consider if all time is now esoterically speaking, then time as you know it is just a construct. We shall say to you that in past times of earlier civilisations that followed planetary alignments with much greater detail, they were possibly nearer the truth than many of you are today. If we whittle this down further, we shall say that this construct is caught up in interplanetary grids that contain the pull between two opposing vibrational variants. It has been determined that all such grids lead back to Source.

If we now consider the esoteric realms and the great living library where your experiences are catalogued and relate this to no time, we shall see that in clearing, as you explain past times through incarnational experience, you not only affect the life and perception of life you find yourself in today, but you affect previous experiences. That is to say you allow more light into the higher being of self. That is the higher concept of self that evolves, incarnation after incarnation. We also wish to announce that many from the inner realms are incarnated here now, at this time of no time. In taking on such embodiment, you have the understanding of how this may aid the planet and its life form to evolve, thus affecting all of creation and the evolutionary process along its continuum.

We have introduced certain keys within a set named 'the higher self' to aid such a process for all sentient life. This ensures sentient life has a clear connection to the divine and in doing this we present the key of the clarion call. This key initiates the process of self, back into service of the light and Source. It reconnects you with the divine and clears a path of connection to the light and a reminder that you are never away from Source. The second key of this set includes the sentient mission key. This unlocks memories of why you incarnated and the mission you decided to seek to undertake. This key may be used for clarity at differing times along the path, as on completion of one aspect of the journey a new challenge may then be set. The third key in this set is the key named the key to the higher self. This key is used to ensure a clear connection between Source, the higher self and the incarnation of embodiment. We shall now discuss the higher self within this text.

The higher self is the aspect of the soul that grows as a result of the lessons learnt. The higher self was born through creation of a life form in an incarnational experience, and by that we mean that the higher self is the aspect of the soul that follows a sentient through every embodiment. It is this aspect of self that remains in esoteric realms. If we dig further into this concept, we see that on the creation of a new soul there is a soul essence, which is whole and complete at the time of creation with differing aspects that no other soul holds. So, Source decided there needed to be a way in which the sentient being in embodiment could relate to the esoteric realms of existence in which the higher self was created. The higher self was created so that all beings could not forget who they are. If we look at animal life, we shall come to an understanding that they too have a higher aspect of self, as within the term beings we incorporate animal life. We mention this for all those working with the animal kingdom upon this planet and remind you that if they have suffered during life they will also have blocks within their energy field.

You might ask whether the animal realm reincarnate and we say to you they do, and in the esoteric realm they have their own journeys to contemplate. Do not be surprised if your pet has been attached to you before as animal life is given to sentient life as a gift. This gift is also teaching sentient life lessons, as it is in the treatment of an animal many lessons can be learnt. We shall go back to the early tale of the dog who had been abused and inform you that if the dog turns on sentient life, there is much to be learnt by the owner should indeed they choose to reflect on how they treated the animal. The animal also grows from this and this leads back into harmonic resonance nicely, as we see the energy of animals feed into the consciousness of a planet. That is to say that within the inner spheres they have such a depth of understanding about life forms and vibratory rates that animals are treated with the upmost respect. Within these spheres, all understand that if animals are indeed treated with negative patterning, this affects the planetary grids which surround them. As all in the inner spheres work for the collective good, rarely do you see an animal abused.

We discuss this now to remind you that all life is part of creation. We extend this teaching to your farmed animals and wildlife as all were given as gifts, if only you open your eyes. Do not think that the spider or rat do not aid your kind! We say to you that the spider was given to keep the flies at bay and if you notice the intricate patterns within a spider's web and their beauty, much can be learnt from this. They hold some key aspects of life and geometric patterning's that are worth a closer look. The rats of which we speak were given a bad name due to your history and rumours of the bubonic plague. We say to you that the governmental structures at that time needed something to blame for such disease, and the rats and the fleas seemed the perfect deterrent. Has anyone considered that this spread of disease may have been caused by sanitation issues. Sanitation issues that sentient life failed to address due to greed and the class systems that were found in that era. Today, in western worlds, this is no longer such an issue, however within the continents deemed as third world, such issues remain. In many of these regions we see wealth and luxury for those in power, however we draw your attention back to epidemics like the plague to inform you that such power over other sentient life forms will cease as the collective consciousness raises within your realm of existence. Source has decreed this, so many monumental changes will be seen in the future.

Those of you with doubt that Creator holds such powers to decree such change have much to learn and remember. Again, there remains no judgement on those sceptical of the prime force behind creational forces. Such changes will be instigated out of the supreme love for all sentient life. How does this fit into the concept of free will, many will utter? We say to you that those suffering in such a way are not able to exert their free will during their incarnation. If we review the chapter containing The War of the Worlds we see the consequence of such power. Did the sentient beings volunteer for such hardship? In part, they chose such embodiment, as many of you have in past incarnations. They did not choose the lack of ability to move from suffering into becoming who they truly are. We say this to you so that you may explore the concept of suppression of sentient life. To move into the golden age such suppression will cease. All of creation is carefully planned within the esoteric realms and as a planet shifts its vibration the collective must follow. As more become conscious much oppression will collapse, truths will be highlighted, and the masses will speak.

Back to the rats who, in fact, give the environment much aid as they clear up other life forms. If they were eradicated this may jeopardise much life and this brings us to mention voles. Voles belong to the rat family, and if these little fury balls became extinct then specific plant life would fail to replicate. Within the rat's family genetic make up there lays a cellular structure that attracts certain plant life to continue to grow, due to the mastication process of the rat and the enzymes produced. This is worth research. Many animal groups have specific effects on the environment that have not yet been realised. Source brings this knowledge to your planet now, so you consider all creation. We have expressed before that there is no mistakes in creation, Source made all of creation from love.

Back to the concept of the higher self and the twin flame connection. Source, being the alpha and the omega, decreed that on birthing a soul there would be both the alpha and omega aspects and so, two aspects of the same soul were created. That is to say that the soul become two parts of a whole, one carrying aspects of the omega, one of the alpha. We again draw your attention back to the concept of the twin flame and state very clearly that it is not who you are in a relationship with, but the lessons each relationship provides. We discuss all relationships within this analogy, whether that be romantic or otherwise. We ask that the emphasis is taken off the twin flame and placed upon lessons learnt by the souls. In the inner realms they understand the concept of duality within creation and they do not sit and question the twin flame aspect, as all know that tremendous gains come from all relationships which they find themselves in.

Many will now question the probability of this. We say to you that in all life there are two aspects that hold specific characteristics. If we take plant life, we see both forms in the main. Within the animal kingdom there remain a few animals that do not require a partner as due to extinction becoming a prospect some are able to birth through parthenogenesis. Source created parthenogenesis so that certain life forms would not die out within your realm as they aid much planetary existence. We again postulate that Source has created all beings from love and that the alpha lives on, and as such the male of a species may be residing in a different space-time continuum or realm of existence. We again discuss whether this may be so within the twin flame relations and this matters not. The animals did not board the Ark in twos for no reason, again much of this story has failed to be understood. The rationale for this was to remind your life form of the duality of existence. The duality of the alpha and omega, the light and the dark, the differing vibrational resonance. This is the part of creation this message was trying to impart. Duality remains in most walks of life such as night and day and duality is seen in every realm of existence, including the inner planes. If we appraise duality, we understand that it is the duality of the incarnated existence we wish you to work upon. By this we mean that in the clearing of old stories we set a new vibrational resonance that is from the light, free from many blocks. The light is what all hope to become, known or unknown. We all strive to become one with Source the father, mother of creation itself, the life force that keeps the breath in the body connected through the higher self.

The higher self is therefore the vessel that remains in the esoteric realm, the higher guide to the individual embodiment in which you find yourselves. When you clear the stories of incarnations, the stories that held you back from the realisation of who you are, you also clear the blocks held within the higher aspects of the soul. This higher aspect remains in the esoteric realm, held within one of the many minds of the Creator. We discuss the many minds of Creator, so you may realise that you are never truly disconnected from Source, regardless of the place in which you incarnate. You may liken this analogy to the many areas of your brain in trying to grasp an understanding and much about the brain remains unknown. We discuss the unknown as there remain many aspects of creation and Creator that are not understood within the earthly realm. We shall now explore an area that is greatly misunderstood on the planet and it is that of judgements. In the esoteric spheres such judgements are not passed by Creator itself, but by the aspects of the creators you and me that walk the incarnated planes. We have discussed that all creations come from love, in the knowing all would cease to be without the duality of existence. This will now be contemplated in greater depth.

Chapter 14

The Power of Judgement, Enlightenment and The Keys

Who can define the word judgement with a total understanding of the construct of such a word? We say none of you, and that is why we wish to include this within the writings we bring. Judgement has multifaceted interpretations. We first will examine the concept of being judged. What is this but some belief that others know what is right. We say that it is a vibrational resonance of darker energy, blocks if you like, that make others judge another being. With this we include judgements about the way someone looks, or presents themselves, judgements about what someone has or has not, judgements about career choice or lack of career choice. Let us tell you that through many incarnations just like those that you judge in such a way, you have also been judged in such a way. We again examine the incarnation experience and explain this in the way of a short vignette.

We see a beautiful young model who has wealth and a following, she lives her life in the bright lights of the city. She is very condescending of those that carry a little extra weight around their middle. When we look back to one of her many incarnation we see this same soul, terribly large, and then we take you back to the potato famine of 1800s and discuss how before the famine and potato blight hit the land she was a very large chef working for the well-known gentry. Can you imagine her stirring her big black pot over the open fire? Plump and large, her round cheeks all aglow. Judged as the buxom bellower by many of the staff who worked in this abode, large and full of hot air. The events that followed were terrible for man and beast, and so the local gentry had to let her go. Having never married she found herself alone in the world, and where her waist was once round and squashy, it now was thin, and her ribs showed through. She lived hand to mouth and found herself in rotten squalor. She became very bitter about the hand she was dealt, blaming God and others, and the rest, as they say, is history. The poor soul died and returned home all alone, cold and hungry.

We examine this tale to get a greater understanding of how this plays out in the scenario she now finds herself. She is holding on to a past belief that she was abandoned and alone. She subconsciously associates being large around the waist with many judgements made upon her that she felt within her soul, nicknames that hurt and bruised her pride. She views those with little and unable to contribute to society with disdain, as she was left abandoned and alone. You may now be wondering why such an event occurred in the first place. We say again such events as the potato blight occurred due to the greed of man, squabbles over land ownership and the way more money could be made. They failed to see the bigger picture, shall we say, and grow enough crops to sustain the people of the land, and what was grown and bred was often exported by the gentry. Again, we examine the tyranny within systems that negate the way that societies live.

We now draw your attention to other judgements, and of this we talk about how you judge yourselves against judgements made against another. We often smile, esoterically speaking, when we hear you utter the words, 'I would never do that' and 'Oh, how terrible.' Let us categorically state that you have done all those things and more. If we say to you that many have incarnated again and again in your realm to learn lessons, and such lessons enable you to remember who you truly are. Jeshua informed you all about forgiveness, but the masses could not hear. So, tales became misconstrued and reconstructed to suit the masses. No judgement is made on this, pardon the pun once again dear readers, however the message was that of hope. When we discuss hope in this context, it is to impart that the hope was that many would hear and review the patterns they kept repeating through incarnations. The patterns of judgement of another. Many masters imparted such truths, many did not hear. Judge not or be judged. In judgement we fail to see repeating patterns in ourselves. How many reading this are now a little affronted, believing they don't judge others? How many can tell me you never judged the drinker, the smoker, the destitute gambler? How many have never judged the prostitute, sexuality or skin colour of others? How many haven't judged the friend, the neighbour, the police? How many of you don't judge the judges, the social workers, the doctors and nurses or the lawyers? How many of you don't judge the film star, the boy next door, the cleaner and the road sweeper?

We say none of you and all of you. You have all made such judgements and many more throughout the embodiment processes. We ask that the path is cleared so a new resonance may infuse the planet. A new harmonic resonance of love light. Such love light will be discussed within the next chapter. Back to judgement, and we enlighten you by saying much judgement is based upon fear, and in examining the earlier tale we will see such correlation. Judgements are often cast from fear, fear of persecution, fear of being alone, fear of ending up the same way, fear of others, fear of being judged as you judge others, fear of the known and unknown, fear of being less than the next man, fear of someone overtaking you, pipping you to the post! We could continue on the subject of fears that control your societies and norms that make you act in a certain way. This would be futile to mention, unless a solution to all this fear was being offered. The solution lies with you, dear ones, the reader and the enlightened, those that are awake to a new way of being. In recognition of this trait running through your vibrations, we hope that you will begin the work to stamp out such fears. Again, we remind you of the many tools on the planet to aid this change in vibrational resonance. We remind you that in doing so, more of the planet can clear the grids in and around, and earth can be welcomed into the bosom of love light.

This brings us nicely to discuss the keys that aid you to clear limiting fears, beliefs and behaviours and we introduce the set of keys known as 'the way to enlightenment.' The first key of the set includes the 'Key of Judgements.' This small round key opens the door to you being able to release the fear of being judged due to judging self. In releasing such fears, it also enables you not to judge others so freely. This key unlocks the potential to look at other's actions with more clarity without the judgements you impose.

The second key in the set is a large jewelled key, the opposite polarity to the previous key as it is named the 'Key of No Judgements.' This will be fully explained in the next paragraph. The final key of the set is the 'Key of Integrity.' This key aids sentient beings to come from a place of integrity. When we whittle down such a word we see this key is integral to change of perceptions, as when fears are cleared, a new resonance must be fully integrated into an energy field. Integrity is a base which all of you should express, in your thoughts, actions, words and deeds. Truth without pain can be very enlightening, as it is the truth that sets you apart from lower vibrational implications. Such implications of mistruths, however small, set a president for your experiences. We say this so it may enlighten you to the fact that in the coming years such mistruths will come to light much quicker than in the past. We see many truths being exposed now within your systems and social structures and media. For a planet to truly ascend, your truths will out. At a vibrational level, the act of telling a mistruth cannot be underestimated. We have discussed actions and reactions and when related to a vibrational resonance we see that such mistruths in action, word, deed and thought resonate at a very low frequency. This feeds into the grid systems that we have discussed earlier and keeps the planet's vibrations lower, it feeds into the tug (ebb), if you will, rather than the pull (flow) towards the light. We remind you of the Universal Laws of Creation and remind you this has been explained in a way which you may understand.

The middle key in the set 'the key of no judgement' has been introduced to set down a new way of thinking about 'what and whom and why you judge.' This key is presented by Source to give you an understanding about the judgements you have made over many incarnations. It brings you back to the love light of Source and reminds you of how such previous judgements have held you back along the path to enlightenment. We discuss enlightenment, for it is truly this you all aim to attain.

Enlightenment through those receiving the keys is a possibility. We shall now discuss enlightenment in the esoteric senses of the word. What is enlightenment? It is the journey back to knowing who you truly are, to remembrance of why you chose embodiment within the space-time continuum in which you find yourself. We have discussed the higher self and how this higher self remains in the esoteric realm and we shall now discuss briefly discuss soul essence. This is the essence of the new soul before any incarnational experience. This essence is placed nearer to creator than the higher self, and is not as malleable and changeable as the higher self. This is the anchor is you like, that connects you always with creator.

Back to the higher self, every soul lesson learnt, however small, leads into a part of the whole. By this we mean that the higher self that remains in the esoteric sphere grows and adapts with each lesson. This continues no matter which realm you incarnate within and we have discussed that within the inner realms lessons remain, they are just very different experiences. To quantify would be impossible as you would not be able to contemplate such lessons with the understanding which they deserve. By the growth of the higher self, we see a much stronger connection with the Creator, lines are cleared, if you will. If we liken this to a telephone line and review the early days of the formation of such a tool within your realm, we see it full of crackles and blocks. We wish you to review the aspect known as the higher self in such a light, and we say to you that the more old stories you clear, the clearer the connection, the more crackle and blocks are released. This next fable highlights how the clearing of such crackles and blocks allows more joy in embodiment, more light to stream through the higher aspects of self, and a greater connection to the love of Source.

There was once an old widow whose name was not known, but around the world she did roam. She came to a place full of joy, this very fact made her cry. For she had never been happy you see, she was too busy, she could not see the beauty before her. So please heed this tale, she spent many a year chasing her tail. In the chase, this way and that, she forgot why she came here, and that's where she fell flat. She lived in the past and this fact is true, she made judgements you see about this and that, she made judgements of self and that kept her flat. Those judgements of self included such facts, that she was not there for her husband, her neighbour, her cat. She failed to support him through hard times and good, she was always judging his actions and putting him down, it really did make him frown. She truly did make him feel the clown. She judged his judgements, she judged the house, she blamed him for their lack of wealth. She judged the neighbours for the lifestyle they led, she judged the cat for forsaking the bed. The bed she had bought and it failed to choose. The cat deserted the house for a life on the move. She ended up sad and alone, as the cat was not the only thing that had flown. Flown the nest and this fact is true, the husband, the neighbour, all felt blue, when around the old lady whose name is not known. So now she judges herself this fact remains known. She judges herself for what could have been, she sits with regrets and her bottle of gin. Her past deeds have punched her real hard on the chin. When stumbling on this place full of joy, she remembered her deeds and that made her cry. Cry for the judgements she made, the judgements of others that had kept her a slave. As the place which she stumbled, there on that day, had cleared all past issues of judgements they made.

So, this place was now filled with glee, all people rejoicing, more love light you see. All the souls had come out of the cave, the cave of self-judgements that had kept them enslaved. The resonance of love had over taken the place, gone was the past that kept them flat on their face. They welcomed in this old soul you see, they welcomed her to join them with a new jolly glee. They helped her clear up the judgements of self and come to terms with the facts she didn't own a big house. They opened her heart this is true, they opened her heart so she didn't feel blue. She rejoiced with them, she rejoiced all day long, and she settled down here where all judgements had gone. She has a new cat, a house with a log fire, and a new chap whose joyful, witty, and stands in his power. The tale of this story it's true to impart, that things may change dramatically when clearing the past. The future is brighter, becomes full of glee, the glee spreads to others and that is, you see, the place we all wish to be. So please dear reader, do take heed, when judgements are cast upon this or upon that, you are judging yourself and that's where you fall flat. Clear up such issues in which way you choose, slip on a new pair of shiny shoes. Dance with the new joy which you'll find in your hearts, have faith in future, don't dwell in the past. Live with joy in the moment called now. So, in concluding this tale, we discuss clearing the judgements that no longer serve, not the judgements that keep you vibrating lower than you truly deserve.

    The greater light you receive and exude within your incarnational experience the greater peace you feel. The vaster your light, the greater the prospect of your ability to aid others reach such light. The further that the light you hold feeds into the higher consciousness of the world which you inhabit. The clearer the grids to let more love light in within and around, the closer you become to Source energy, the resonance of Om and love. We conclude this chapter by referring to this word love – love is a feeling you all strive to experience. We shall now review love in the highest sense of the word.

Remarkable Misdeeds Key Set

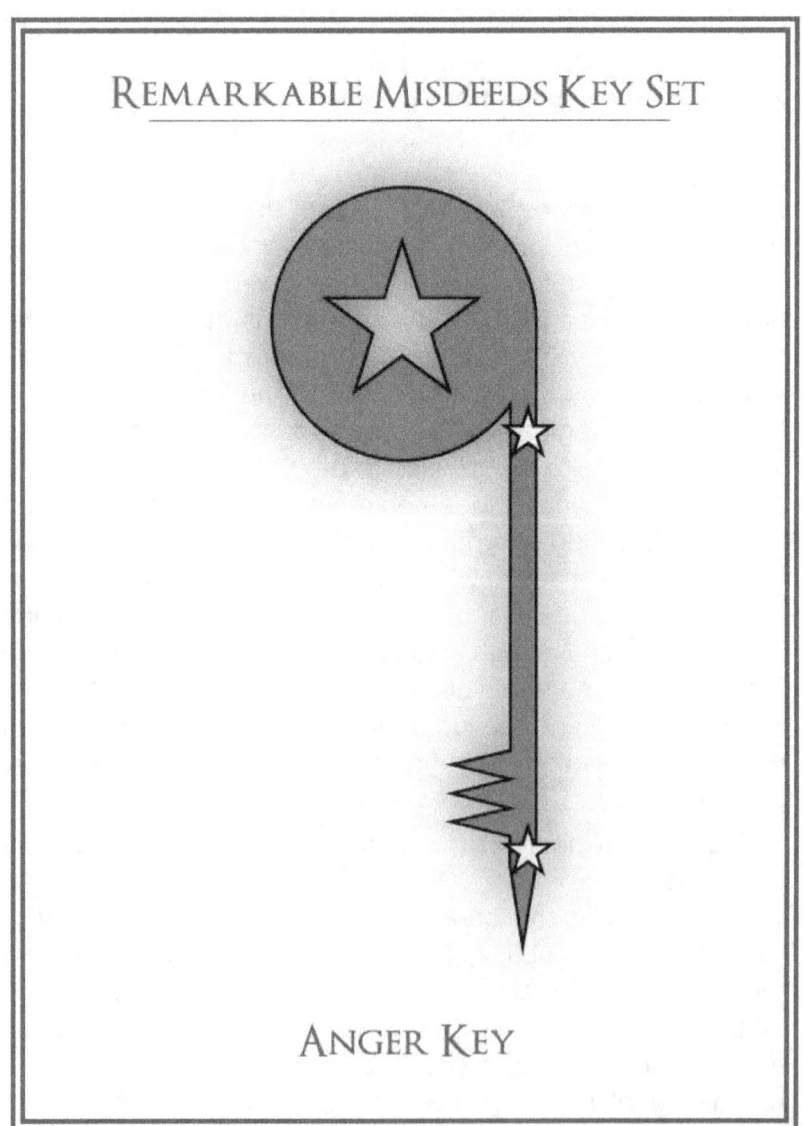

Anger Key

Chapter 15

Love and The Keys

Love is the essence of creation. The force behind all there is. The vibrational sound of love is Om. The sound that reverberates throughout creation itself. We introduce here a very important set of keys, so you can have a greater depth of understanding of this word. The word of Creator and creation love.

Om has been debated by many religious fractions and included in many teachings upon your planet for good reason, as it truly contains the highest vibrational essence, that of love. It has been mentioned throughout your histories and some of the earliest esoteric texts discuss this resonance. This sound can be depicted as the breath of Creator, creating creation. It is breath we shall now discuss.

Breathing is a part of universal creation within all realms of existence as breath is given as a gift so you may continue an incarnation. The same is true within all the universes which have come under much review in this book. All sentient beings require the breath of life; the breath of life is a precious gift for you, from Creator. We mention this within this chapter as it is within the breath of life many answers can be found. By this we mean, if you took a breath and examined a tree, how many would see the tree in all its glory? Many would rush past taking the breath of life unconsciously, never pausing to see the beauty around. Many are caught up in whirlwind that has become existence and we say to you, this is the crux of many problems upon your planet, that and greed, the 'must have' culture you find yourselves in. This culture has been viewed esoterically speaking along a continuum, we shall call it a timeline of existence amongst many timelines of creational forces that exist.

To examine this concept further, we shall go back a few million years before the creation of your planet, back to the inner realms and the first sound of creation; Om. Om reverberated around the empty planes of existence that existed in eternity, the breath of Creator blew into the great expanse of emptiness that was soon to be filled with the love that Source held in every cell, thought, action, word and deed. We discuss this in this context, so you may understand that Creator is unlike anything you can and will comprehend, however, if you can imagine this space of no time, this great empty expanse of vibrating matter void of thought, action, deed, some may build up a picture. We continue to say that the vibration of love was therefore breathed into existence and this is all you need to know. We state this fact as you may ponder on this and on that, but it has no relevance to the fact that your life force breath was given to you as a gift. We have determined that in creation there must be two opposing forces duality, and it is this we now truly wish to explore. Duality is a construct born out of love for creation, we have previously determined. To keep creative forces in play, it requires such an ebb and flow. This is true of many aspects of creation, and it is the vibration of love that we wish now to examine.

We have determined that certain sounds hold a higher vibrational pull towards the light, the light of love, the crux of creation. We shall now examine deeds, thoughts and actions that come from love. It is this state that you wish to attain, known or unknown. We discuss this in relation to ascension and state that to move, as a planet, back towards the all important love light and the breath of Source, requires many to be singing from the same resonating essence and that is the essence of love.

Love is often viewed within your realm and measured by who loves whom. How many friends you have. It is on a relationship level that many discuss the term love. Love of life has made a recent revival, as many now review abundance and speak of joy. Is it truly understood, this word love? Love is the beginning and the end, the alpha and the omega, it is the glue, it shines down from your sun, it is the hot and the cold that blows through your land, the wind and the rain. It is the waves crashing against the shores, it is the dark of the night, it is the butterfly floating by, it is the chirp of bird song at the start of the day. It is the grass blowing in the wind, it is the rustle of autumn leaves. It is in this and in that, it is all around, if only you could see.

We write this now, not to detract from those of you that are living in a state of suffering, but to remind you all of the love in everything all around. When you start to give thanks for such beauty of creation then you can truly begin to live. It is in the appreciation of beauty, thanks and analysis of the concept of love that true healing can really be felt. Again, we mention that as you clear blocks that have held you back from such appreciations, you are able to attain the joy and love which many hope to reach. When this joy is attained, you will see your relationships blossom and bloom, as it is the love you exude from within yourself that really leads you to the joyous path of discovery to which many of you aspire.

Many block the negative vibrations within by turning to certain substances available to you in your lands. By that we mean numbing and suppressing of past hurts, lack of real joy through the use of alcohol, cannabis, drug taking behaviours and cigarette smoking. The list can go on, but their use remains the same. They are used to escape the reality in which you live. We draw your attention back to the story of the women who joined her husband in their local watering hole, and the rest is history as she became reliant on the source. The source of her demise from knowing who she truly was.

We are not detracting from the ancestral and cellular addictive patterning that holds a resonance within the cellular memories. We are also not judging why such occurrences remain prevalent within your realm, as in the esoteric sphere we watch your struggles with much gratitude. This may sound a contradiction of sorts. However, we have previously discussed how many in the outer spheres are held in great esteem as they are quite literally keeping the cosmos afloat! We remind you again that many volunteer for such experiences in the knowing that without them, creative life forces as we know them would cease to be. So, in inhabiting such an outer realm planet, the wheels of creation keep turning as incarnation after incarnation, in the time of no time, you walk the path back to the remembrances of who you truly are. When reviewed in this context you are indeed great beings of light, the masters and teachers in the tomorrow of eternity. We use the term tomorrow loosely as it is today we wish you to concentrate on, this minute in time you find yourself reading this text. We once again add a story within a story to highlight love in its truest form.

We wish to take you back to a time that time forgot. A time of no time, where all journeys are, knowingly, mapped through experience, and of this we talk of the inner realms of existence. Within the inner realms, many, many moons ago, we saw a young sentient being starting out on her journey of discovery. At this time, many of the Laws of the Universe were being discovered and understood by those in incarnation, and in this story we wish to examine the Law of Reciprocity. This law is about reciprocal lessons and it is the lessons regarding love we shall now review.

Everything is created from love. This has been established throughout this book. Within the inner realms, just as you are learning today, love was being reviewed by the sentient beings and many were debating this creative force. The young sentient in question had many friends and her parents were attached to those in high places. This made the young sentient feel very grandiose, a little big for her boots is the term that comes to mind. She decided that love held a great power, as she saw those in power expressing love in many of their actions. It was drilled into her that love was the glue that held all things, interactions and friendships together. In this they forgot to teach that love must be heartfelt, and actions and words must marry up.

She was a dear loving soul but sadly forgot that words and deeds must come from loving intent and so she went out one day to meet some of her chums and they stumbled across a vast lake. By the lake there lived an old wise soul who had been known as one of the elders. Little did they know, this old soul was ready to return home in the esoteric sense of the word. The young girl felt thirsty so knocked on the old soul's door requesting refreshment. The old soul was only too happy to oblige, but whilst in her abode the young soul stumbled across some old papers and decided they looked interesting. She took these old scrolls and placed them in her bag. The old soul sent her on her way with fruits from the garden and the young soul reciprocated by hugging the old soul and thanking her for her kindness.

The scrolls were not missed by the elder for some time. She noticed they had gone when she came to have a meeting with some of the higher council of light where she intended to pass on the very important research she had completed on the esoteric understanding of some of the Laws of the Universes. In noticing them missing she became distraught as she had spent many a moon constructing the data. The council, on hearing of such an event, began questioning the old soul and, being in direct contact with Source energy, they were pointed in the direction of the missing scrolls. The council paid a visit to the family abode of the young soul and questioning ensued. The young soul denied the visit to the elder's abode and exclaimed they must be mistaken. The council understood that such denial came from fear, and so they took the young soul on a journey. A journey where she was surrounded by love, compassion and bathed in peace and serenity. They took her on an adventure to the most beautiful place in the cosmos at that time, the garden of the blossoming love. She felt so nurtured in this place that she examined her actions and came to a deep understanding about reciprocal relations. By this we relate that reciprocity must come from a place of heartfelt love. In this place of beauty and peace, she reflected with love on why she took such actions, as in response to generosity she had reacted with deceitful intent due to nothing more than curiosity. Due to her inner soul being filled with love, compassion and serenity, the young soul felt enabled to tell the truth and instead of shame, she was taught that with love, compassion and understanding and a sense of peace, all misdeeds could be rectified. The papers were returned to the elder so she could share her wisdom with the masses, and this is a story that remains told within the inner realms frequently, so the young can appreciate the power of love and the reciprocal power of love from the heart.

This has been included within these teachings as it has some relevance to the keys on offer at this time. This tale could have had a very different ending if the young soul in question had been abolished for her curiosity, shutting down her need to explore the realm in which she lived. She would have consequently gone on to have a feeling of not loving herself, as shame would produce a block within her energy field. Within the inner spheres this is inherently known, partly due to the experience of the young soul. We mention that creation was in the early stages, and it is from this tale that Creator decided that further keys would be introduced to aid all sentient life within all spheres of existence, no matter where incarnating. We again relay that the keys are not in use in many of the outer realms as the energy of such planes could not hold the resonance of such keys. The understanding and velocity would be too great for the sentient to receive, as they are a work in progress. By this we mean they are at work to remember who they truly are and the energy surrounding them is too blocked and stagnant to assist them at the point in the eternal continuum in which they find themselves. Here, we refer to the timelines in which they are travelling, and this will be discussed in greater depth within the next chapter.

Reciprocity is indeed a concept which all strive to attain, maintain and comprehend in the highest sense of the word. Reciprocity is a construct seen in all relationships, between all fractions. It has also been upheld upon your planet within the duality of existence, and by this we refer to the lower ways in which reciprocity plays out within relationships. If we look at power within the relationships in which you find yourselves, we see reciprocity in the lower sense of the word. An example of such would be within family structures and the play for power, so one family member sees the need to exert control over another by putting down their actions. What is really required to address such an issue is love and compassion for the other's journey.

If we take the example of a longstanding feud between a mother and a son and examine it from the angle of reciprocity, we see in many ways the play for power with one member trying to gain control over another. Let us examine such an example further. It may transpire that back in the beginning, before the soul incarnates, that one parent did not wish for a child so soon after marriage. The birth of the child led to a breakdown in communication between the parents. Now let us examine how the past affects future events. The parents split up due to the pressures the child placed upon their lives, and the mother felt no strong attachment to the child. As the child grew to a man, she made unreasonable demands on him, tried to control his life and tell him what to do from a place of anger. She had never been able to demonstrate affection towards him and hugs were rare in his early years. The father left and lost contact with the mother and child, so compounded with the lack of attachment, the child felt abandonment. In his twenties the man marries, and the mother feels a lack of attachment to the partner whom he picks. She criticises this and that, as she always has, making the son feel inadequate.

This was a pattern she was repeating as for generations this parenting style had ensued.

This learnt behaviour further impacted on the reciprocal relationship between the pair, until one day the son had enough and told his mother she was cruel and unloving. The mother became mad, as this accusation brought up memories of the departure of her husband and, being stubborn, she told the son not to contact her again. He decided this was for the best as the relationship they shared made him feel low and due to this the son wasn't really able to love himself. Many of the comments cut him to the core. They now became distant, stuck in a feud through nothing more than the lack of reciprocity. No reciprocity for generations, and the impact of early events and planning caused much pain, lack of joy and blocks within the energy field. We introduce the keys of love to clear up such issues so that the sentient journey may be fuelled with more joy and appreciation for the great gift called life.

The first key we introduced is named the key of love. It is a pink key with a heart and this clears up many issues about the lack of love a being may find for themselves. It also clears a path for them to become more loving towards one another. The second key is that of compassion and omits a pink etheric glow. This key clears the energy field of lack of compassion for self and also others. So, it enables a sentient to have greater compassion for another's journey. The third key in the set lays down a new resonance, that of peace and serenity and when used in conjunction with other keys it brings in a sense of overwhelming calm in many given situations. All keys within the set enable a sentient to evolve in their understanding of reciprocity and love in the truest sense of the word, and that word is, 'a clear path to Source through the higher self, so all actions and reactions are examined with a greater velocity towards loving dispositions.' This clears away much stagnating energy from the soul in embodiment, and again enables more light to filter through to the realm of existence called earth.

We discuss earth now as much stagnant energy is being transmuted and many relationships may be terminated as many find a new way of being. This is not to be judged, as it is correct for each sentient being to be able to learn lessons that have been playing out through history. We remind you of the fact that many will transform beliefs, and many may struggle in this embodiment. This is correct for each soul, as their journey is based upon their evolutionary process, the journey of remembering who they truly are. This brings us nicely to the next chapter where timelines will be examined.

Possibility of Perception Key Set

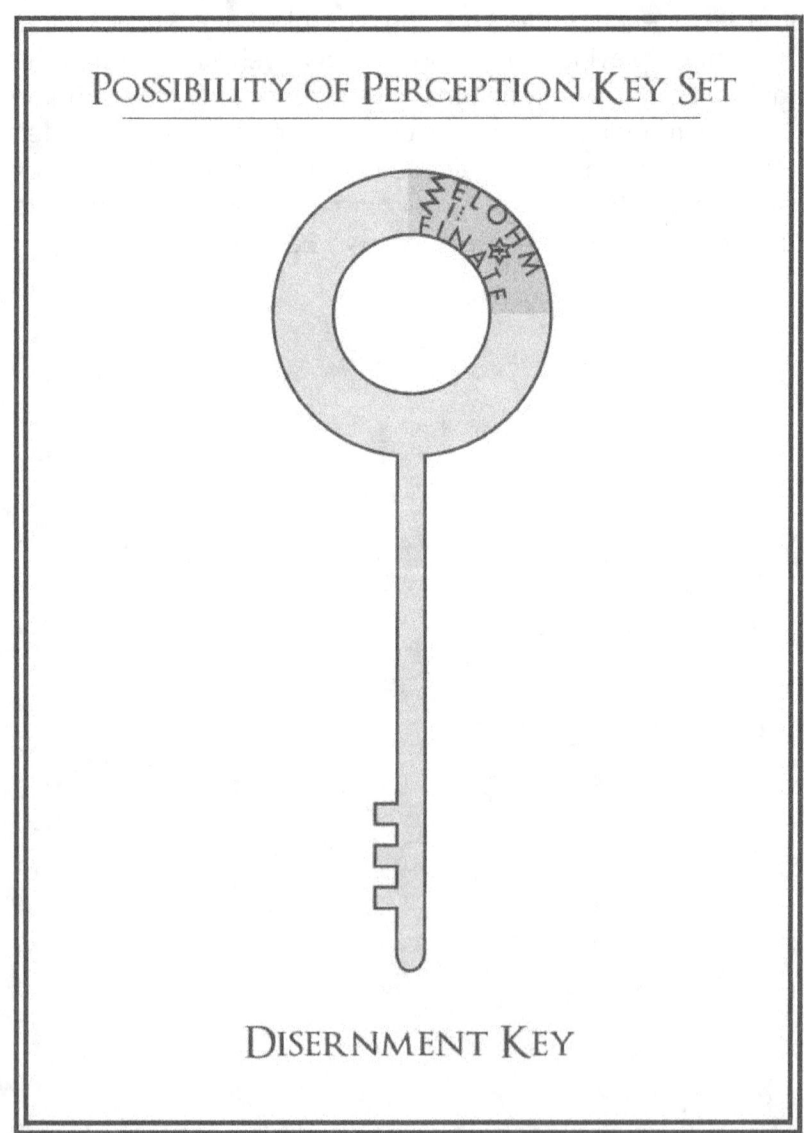

Disernment Key

Chapter 16

Inter-dimensional Timelines and The Keys and the Journey Back to The Higher Self

Timelines are a complex phenomenon of which little is known. Timelines originate from the time of earliest creation when Source required a means to contain the ebb and flow of the universes. We previously discussed how in the beginning of the creation of the inner realms, a contrast was required to maintain sentient life. By this we discussed duality and remind you again of the duality seen throughout existence. We discussed the pull between subatomic particles and state again, not for effect but to get the very salient point across, that without this pull between fractious groups all would cease to be. We take you back to the first breath of creation and remind you of a state of no matter, the first resolutely mass was that which carried the vibration of love.

However, from the first cell of creation, Creator discovered there required a certain ebb and flow to maintain homeostasis. When reviewing this at a macro level, for all life to maintain a homeostatic revolutionary potential, there must be opposing gravitational forces at play. There must be higher and lower vibrational rates that ensure the movement of potential from one line to another, or all would cease to be. To aid Creator maintaining the ebb and flow, timelines were introduced, to support sentient life to continue through planes of existence. We discuss these planes and timelines not in the esoteric sense, as this is completely different concept, but within the embodiment process.

So, incarnation after incarnation, within certain realms of

existence, timelines are keeping the sentient from skipping certain lessons that they choose to incarnate to learn. If we examine the early man, the Neanderthals, we can assume they were on a lower timeline than you are today. Let us say they are on a timeline that enables them to understand the basic concepts of life. The need for food, the need to hunt, the need to drink, without the cognitive functions of the higher mind. The lessons they came to embodiment to learn are those which require basic skill sets in order to maintain life. They did, however, learn about working together to maintain an existence, and as they progressed through various stages of embodiment, new lessons were laid down which required differing genetic make up. We now see the rise of early man. So, there is a shift from a lower frequency existence of the Neanderthals, to a higher form of embodiment in the human form we see today. We discuss the timelines as inter-dimensional as there are many dimensions to existence.

If we break this down further, the dimensional aspect becomes quite complex. In lay terms we wish you to know that to become more enlightened takes a shift in cognition and it is this that we speak of when discussing a timeline shift. We discuss lower dimensional timelines and wish to give an example so you, the reader, may understand. For this we journey backwards to the early times in creation within the inner realms, when such timelines became a necessity. This was due to some sentient life incarnating with great knowledge in the esoteric sense. This was deemed necessary by Creator, as there were still planetary disputes as previously mentioned. Creator needed strong leaders and masters, so the life here would not fall into lower duality existence. This needed to be measured in a way, and so timelines were created as a way of measuring the path of enlightenment, to keep track, if you will, on the masters and those less informed. Those incarnating with specific esoteric understanding had to be monitored, as they continued to evolve into a greater aspect of themselves. We have determined their lessons are very different from those we find within the outer realms. Some masters remain in the esoteric spheres in order to aid creation and those in embodiment, as this is their mission to do so. It is worth noting that within the inner spheres that those incarnating have a much wider understanding and connection to the esoteric realms and therefore life is lived between the duality of incarnation and the esoteric spheres.

Timelines within planetary structures are also required to maintain the homeostasis we previously discussed. As all planets have a living form, they too are able to adjust in a dimensional capacity, just like sentient life. If we review a planet's lay lines, for example, and view them as the veins and arteries that run through the human form, we can understand how blockages have disrupted the outer layers of the earth. We give this analogy, so you may understand the concept of planetary life and how lower dimensional frequencies may affect such life. We take you back to chapter five and the story of the young key keeper who incarnated on the planet known as Astonia. We see an example of the effect of the veins and arteries clearing too quickly and the floods that ensued as way of exempla. We remind you that this structure has been laid down, so planets are able to monitor where they are on the dimensional grid. That is to say, much like the sentient being's ability to shift to a higher consciousness, this is also true of a planet.

Many in the lower spheres have not been able to grasp the concept that the realm in which they walk is indeed a form of life. Many have walked upon the land without conscious thought of how this great structure, with all its beauty and glory, came into existence. They walk on the lush grass, unconscious. They swim in the warm seas, unconscious. They fly in the atmosphere surrounding, unconscious. Unconscious that planets are alive, filled with the breath of the great Creator, Source of all there is. Within the inner spheres we state this would never be so. The planets receive the same love and appreciation as all sentient life, and before any actions are taken that may adversely affect the place in which they have been gifted to reside, thought, great thought, is given to the way this may affect their beautiful gift; the planet on which they reside.

Within the ascension process, the lay lines of the planet raising vibration need careful monitoring. This is done in the esoteric spheres, but we call those reading this text to give greater consideration to their actions and the effect these have in the lands in which they live. We discuss the atomic systems, energy and weapons that have been tested across your land. Can you imagine how this may affect the core of the planet's life? Such harmful processes send out such lower vibrational resonance keeping the lines blocked for many millennia. You see this around the place you call Chernobyl, do not think such event does not affect the inner earth.

We discuss during ascension that the sentient, planet and outer planetary grids need to be in coherence in order for the whole to truly ascend to a differing dimensional reality. We have already debated that to be fully locked into a new existence back towards the love light this must be so. So, what truly is a timeline then? It is a movement of consciousness from one vibrational plane of existence to another. There are many planes of existence, esoterically speaking, that you may incarnate. Within the lower vibrational spheres, volcanic eruptions, tidal waves and the like are a common occurrence because the sentient life is unconscious of their actions and they do not examine in depth their actions and reactions which is a Universal Law and cannot be changed. An action in one land may have a devastating consequence on another and this is a fact world leaders need to embrace for the good of all sentient life. We have discussed how your planet is moving dimensionally and this will not be thwarted this time as Source has decreed this, so many dramatic events and changes will be seen within your realm within the next few years. Alongside this shake up of lower vibrational patterning, many more discoveries will come to light for the greatest good of all and many will shift in consciousness. Those that do not will reach a point where such change becomes inevitable as they will not be able to live within the new energies they find themselves. Consciousness will shift and, taking you back to chapter three, this is staggered so the awakenings do not overwhelm the inter and outer planetary structures and grids. Those of you reading this are the informed, in years to come many will look back at this time in history in awe at the lack of awareness in the esoteric sense.

The keys have been introduced now at this time as a means to enable sentient life to move a dimensional timeline, a step forward towards living with greater consciousness. Not just in the esoteric sense but here, in the incarnational experience, transforming old patterns and ways of being, changing action and reactionary experiences for those around. Bringing in greater love light from Source, and in so raising planetary dimensional experience, aiding ascension back towards the light and resonance of Om. The vibration of love.

An example of such keys will now be discussed as a way of illustrating and illuminating timeline shifts and we shall discuss how this the key set is to be known as 'the higher self.' The higher self is the part of your soul essence, held within the esoteric spheres. We discuss this set as we wish to point out that in the esoteric spheres timelines are also prevalent. We shall discuss the timeline of the higher self and, much like inter and outer planetary grids, the higher self can hold higher or lower vibrational form. By this we mean that the more a sentient is able to clear the issues and lessons from embodiment, keeping the wisdom without the distress and nuances of lower vibrational energies, the clearer the higher self. The clearer the higher self, the more a sentient is connected to Source energy, and like many creational currents, the greater the connection to 'the mission' a soul has chosen to incarnate to complete. The more in alignment with the mission, the more positive the experience within the incantatory journeying. The mission is described as the objective of the incarnational experience.

Within the outer realms many fail in their mission and this fact leads to a certain unhappy resonance and bitterness. Many look back on their life and feel they did not really accomplish a great deal. This is often because they were pulled from the path of their objective, and due to actions and reactions from themselves and others, failed to fully complete the objective they intended. When we discuss such objectives, we discuss this in the sense of their life goal. If, for example, we take those on the mission to heal, it may be that they completed some of their objectives as they qualified as a doctor, nurse or physiotherapist, the list goes on. They may, however, have had the objective to mix certain modalities of healing to ensure a holistic way of practice. The mainstream meeting the complementary. They may then become firmly entrenched in the medical model and fail, in part, some of their objective. They may be quite happy with the path but feel at the end of the day that there may have been more that they could have done. Living with regret. This concept will be explored within the following segment.

We then take the case of the sentient pushed into a career by a family member because they, the sentient, accepts someone else always knows best. Generational blocks spring to mind. Control and societal norms play a part in the career choice, and let's say due to such pressure, a sentient becomes a science teacher, although their real joy was found in the creative arts. Had they followed a different course of action, they would have found that they were able to channel art that enabled the world to grow, just by the beauty they experienced when viewing such an expression. The sentient retired and took back this objective in a diluted form as a hobby, never really feeling they were totally happy in career their choice.

We now discuss those who are on a much less fortunate path, as we understand that not all sentient beings within your realm have the same overwhelming possibilities. Would you be able to accept that some sentient beings' objectives were to show others that the world needs to change in behaviour? That such power in certain states destroys lives, and the misdirection of wealth ruins many. We applaud such souls, esoterically speaking, and we call for the masses reading this text to raise vibrational essence, so such atrocities do not occur within this realm for future generations. All beings can sit back and discuss how terrible certain circumstances are, this is true, but how many do anything meaningful to stop such an occurrence. We state again that actions and reactions, cause and effect, must be scrutinised in many of your systems, government structures and establishments. This will occur as Source has decreed it so.

We bring you back to the keys that encompass 'the higher self' set, and state once again that there are three keys that aid a sentient to become in alignment with their incarnational experience. The first key is that of the clarion call, the call back to service of Source, so each mission is completed to ensure the sentient is working for the light. The second key is that of the mission. It enables the soul to have a better understanding to their life course development and points them on the right track, and when stepping into the real objective for incarnation, the sentient is able to be of great service to others. They of course feel much happier, as there are no discrepancies in the thought processes in the working day that keep them unfulfilled. The final key is the key to the higher self, which clears up a channel between the higher self and Source and embodiment, reconnects with the planet and enables the sentient to allow in Source's great love light. All three keys enable a being to step onto a different timeline or have an expanse in consciousness. If they choose to follow their missionary path, they are able to enjoy, to a greater extent, the journey in which they find themselves. This may not be an automatic change of direction but gives the sentient a new resonance, the ability to work towards this possibility, examining differing ways of how this may be achieved along the continuum of the expanse we call incarnational life. It may start with a cheap or low-cost course, there are many roads to reaching an objective, and we hope many can resonate with these words.

We conclude this chapter by reminding you once again, dear reader, to clear the paths, so you may find yourselves living within a new dimensional existence. An existence that leads back to the love light of Source, the great Creator of all things. We ask you to examine the career choices you make and ask you whether they are heartfelt or is there more you wish to accomplish? We offer you this set of keys in order that you may change and grow in the ways of the light. We shall now, within the next chapter, review regret, as it has been touched upon in this chapter, and we introduce the set of keys named 'remarkable misdeeds.'

Chapter 17

Remarkable Misdeeds and The Keys

What is the meaning of a misdeed? A misdeed, viewed esoterically, is an action judged and directed towards yourself. If we examine this concept further, we ask you, the reader, how many of you live with regret? We hear your mumblings about how you wish you had chosen a different path, how you should have stayed here in this country or holidayed there again. We hear you mutter, 'if only I could go back.' Regrets. How they impinge on your existence. We say this now as we wish to examine the concept of living in the past. We discuss this concept in the time of no time, to remind you of the futility of such an existence. As many remunerate about how they could have changed the past, they fail to see the here and now. We give you another little ditty to remind you of how this impacts on your lives and we hope you enjoy this fable.

Down by the strawberry patch there lived a little mouse whose home was watering can. It was warm and cosy for a mouse's house. She roamed about one day, till she came upon a dome, a dome-shaped empty beehive, abandoned and alone. She thought to herself what a lovely home, why is this beehive abandoned and alone?

Now this empty beehive was a good mile from her house, she moved that mile with her husband, the family and the couch. Little mice everywhere a great life they did lead, in the abandoned beehive underneath a tree. Winter turned to spring, summer turned to autumn, when one day a huge farmer decided to stroll in.

'Ah, my abandoned beehive,' why he did exclaim. 'Let me

get that beehive and place it out of the rain. Let me make some money, that would be really swell, money from my honey,' now you see the reason for this tale. The little mice lost their home that day, it was a cold and lonely hour. Mother mouse went on and on, over coming weeks, days and hours.

She moaned and groaned she should have never moved from that discarded watering can, nestled by the leeks. She failed to give thanks for what had been great days, sheltered from the cold, in that discarded beehive and can out of wind and cold. They all moved into a pumpkin after having autumn feasts, it was soggy and smelly, but they did so enjoy that feast. So off they roamed again, mother mouse still moaning about what could have been, forever groaning.

Even where they settled on the banks of river glee, a lovely little home they made from a rocky cavern, underneath a tree. A little haven where no man did roam free to live in glee, underneath the tree, not disturbed by you or me.

A little haven out of the wind and cold. Mother mouse ended all her days complaining still, about her new abode. Hankering for the watering can, wasting time upon the past. Set amongst the leeks in that vegetable patch, within the park. Little did she know that shortly after that, along came a tractor and squashed that can flat. Flat as a pancake, where all lives would have gone back to the Creator to sing a different song.

So, the moral of this tale is do not live in past, it's the future you must live in, live in it with glee, the past may have been bleaker than ever you could see. Here now in the present, that's where we all should be!

We include this tale, so you may now think in a different way, not on what could have been as you may not be in the place you are today. Life could have turned out much bleaker. In living in the past, you are also failing to see the lessons, the lessons you learnt from certain experiences, and where you have now come. The lessons may have been hard or easy, the point is that had you not experienced certain lessons, you would not be able to evolve. Without evolution all would cease to be. So, you see the quandary? Regret does not enhance your embodiment experience; it hinders it greatly. We therefore offer you the key that enables you to clear up such issues of the past, so you may begin to live in the present. The present moment you find yourselves in. Along with this key that we offer, we also offer two more keys in this set. That of resentment and anger. To enable you to live a different tale than that of sorrow and regret.

Resentments differ from judgements in the way that resentments are held within the energy field and have many differing meanings. Resentments embody not only resenting a person, but self, friendship groups, money, wealth, lack of wealth, career, groups, religious fractions, countries and states and the embodiment process. How many reading this have felt resentment towards their parents, for example? Let's say a person moved numerous times in their youth or were sent to boarding school, this could have triggered emotions of sadness and loss. This then sparked a certain rage at being left, or having to move to a new school, hankering after the past and making the individual regretful at what could have been. I could have had lifelong friends, I could have spent many years with my parents. We discuss what could have been again to remind you that had you remained in certain situations your life may have taken a very different route; remember the mouse? Staying in one school, for example, may have meant that you got in with a group that became a gang, or if you stayed with your parents you would have felt unwanted. However, what transpired here was the parents were able to give you much more time and love when they saw you return from boarding school, and you grew up feeling loved not unwanted. We are not saying that all family stories have a happy ending. Some family situations may lead to feelings of abandonment, abuse or neglect. We are saying that living with regret, resentment and anger hinder your path. It is not the story which you wish to forget as this is your story and to forget it would make a mockery of the embodiment process. We are saying that living with such emotional responses to your stories hinders you in the present moment, the moment of now. Such keys offer to clear the emotional baggage you have all not only brought in with you over many incarnations but are experiencing in the here and now. We remind you again that past lives impact on your here and now and remind you of the tale of the model and how her past made her judgemental in the present-day scenarios in which she found herself.

We shall discuss the subject of anger, a most destructive emotion which serves no one, in greater depth, as anger is the force behind many misdeeds. If we take war and atrocity it stems mostly from anger, mixed with a bit of judgement, resentment and the inability to love another as yourself. Anger over which religious fractions holds all the keys, anger over who owns the land, anger over who should be with whom, anger over skin, anger over sexual orientation, anger over this and that. The list could go on. We wish to clear up many such angry, judgemental indoctrinations and point out that to Creator, in creating everything, all is in perfect order. No land belongs to you, no religion belongs to you, no person belongs to you. All is a beautiful part of creation. Perfect in all imperfections.

The imperfection of which we speak is you. As sentient beings within this realm of existence you all decided to label this and that. Such judgements and angry outbursts have nothing to do with Creator or the higher realms of existence directly. Inadvertently of course they do, as they have much to do with Creator maintaining the ebb and flow of existence. So, you see the statement 'creation is perfect with all such imperfections,' just as Creator is pure love, without imperfections nothing would exist. So, we say without judgement over your behaviours, it is time for you as Creator beings to realise your heritage and move back towards the light. A lighter, less dense realm of existence, as Source has determined you have suffered too long and heard your cries.

It is time for movement back to the love light of creation. Within this text we shall discuss the end of the world, the second coming, which a few doctrines and proverbial texts denote. Let us say the time is nigh, again twisted by this soul and that soul to keep the masses uneducated.

The second coming, of which was spoken, is the coming of remembrance, the coming to remembrance of who you truly are. We say again you are all Creator beings and are part of Creator. The Creator of all things. How could this not be so? Do you truly believe a God created these people over here, while a different God created a different lot over there? Who created the planet? This God or that God? Who created the trees? This God or that God? Who created the sky? This God or that God? Creator of all sent many prophets. Who understood? We say again that all religious beliefs lead back to one Creator, Creator of all there is, creating all there is. Creator without judgement, without fear, acting from pure love for all creation. Sorry folks, life is infinite, regardless at this point whether you know it or not. Life has light, life has dark, so do you as part of the one family of Creator. This shall continue, whether on this timeline or that, regardless of your deeds or misdeeds, regardless of your point along the continuum of remembrance.

Back now to anger and how it affects all souls. Within the inner spheres anger remains a probability. It must be stated that there are many tools that aid sentient life to address such problems, and as those in the inner realms truly know who they are, such anger is a rare occurrence. Again, this is not judged in the same way it is within the outer realms, it is aided by all sentient beings involved with another journey, the mission to aid them back to the light. The cause and effect scrutinised, actions and reactions explored, so that the that trigger for the angry event can be given to the light.

Anger within the inner realms is not expressed in the same way. It may be a look or a feeling or another picking up on a fleeting thought. No violence is seen here. We wish to welcome you, the intrepid explorers of the galaxy, back towards this resonance. The resonance of living in the body without the misdeeds that hold you back so. What really are all these emotions if you whittle it down? Where do they come from? We state fear, fear of being pipped to the post. Fear of not living up to societal, family and friend's expectations. Fear of not being the best. Fear that someone is getting more than you or will make it to their destination before you do. Fear that you will not join 'the haves' and shall remain with the 'have nots'. Fear of another's skin, fear of another's choice in partner, fear with sexuality, fear with this, fear with that. Anger is fear; fear of another not doing what you say. Anger comes from control. Anger comes from the lack of control. From where does control stem? Fear. This is the title of the next chapter but for now, we offer the keys again in this time of no time, so that such issues may be addressed. The remarkable misdeeds created for yourselves to experience the incarnated experiences, learn lessons and return to the light. All those within the outer realms strive for this, known or unknown, within the eternal resolutions of what you call life. We look at these experiences and reflect. It is like the sun setting over a lake, glistening sparks reflected on the waters as day turns to night. Little shards of light, dancing on the water, some brighter than others, glistening, none the less in the duality of existence. Source views all light of souls in much the same way and so it is without judgement that we discuss such concepts. It is with love and under the umbrella of Source's love for all the family members that we bring you this text. Onto the next chapter: fear and the dark night of the soul.

Chapter 18

Fear-Based Beliefs, The Keys and The Dark Night of the Soul

Fear is the basis for many misdeeds within your realm. Fear is the darkest vibration of all the vibrational forces in which you can find yourself. Fear drives many heinous acts, although without a degree of this emotive response, all would cease to be. We discuss this in the context of ascension and the ascension process and how fear stagnates inter and outer planetary grids. Fear halts many following the path of the light and bright, fear holds many back from the realisation of whom they truly are. So, we here today to offer the key set named 'the biggest blocks' – the blocks that hold you back. This set includes clearing fears from past, present and changing future timelines in which you may find yourselves. The set also includes self-depreciation and deceit along with joy. We add joy to this set as it is a complete travesty, and therefore a huge block, that many do not live with joy within their souls. We shall now delve into fear-based thoughts with greater velocity, as the key to fear is the velocity at which you fear this and that.

Velocity, what a tremendous word. Examining it within this context we can take velocity to mean the power behind fear. It may be tremendous, it may be miniscule, but fears feed emotional responses in given situations. If we take a husband arguing with another man for looking at his wife with a certain amount of desire and admiration, what do we see? We see the fear within 'the husband', as the viewing of his wife poses a threat to his circumstance. Why is he threatened? Well, it may be a number of reasons, but let us dwell for a moment on the fact that he treats his wife less favourably at times. He takes her for granted, puts her down, not always seeing the shining light his wife brings to his world. So out of fear of loss he turns to anger and becomes abusive towards the other man, threatens him, warns him off like a cockerel clucking over its hens. All that was really required was for him to appreciate his wife, diminishing the fear-led reaction. It may not always be that simple we hear you cry, and while you are quite right, we are not forgetting many differing scenarios that may have caused such a reaction. A reaction generated from fear. There may have been adulterous acts that led the man to behave in such a way, or there may have been ongoing marital issues that made the man feel insecure and live in fear. It is not the point here to go into every possible scenario. He may be running a script of self-depreciation, not believing he was good enough to catch such a pretty young thing. The list goes on. We must not leave out a scenario the other way around, in case gender bias is quoted. We may see a lady, getting on in her years, feeling fear that her partner is about to leave her. She decides to use anger to incite rows that were needless, carried out due to the act of self-depreciation. Self-depreciation will be examined in greater depth as it often plays a part in fear-based reactions, but for now, let's continue upon the notion of fear-based actions.

We may see fears of isolation and see an individual immerse themselves in activities, so they do not spend quality time on their own. This immersion diminishes their ability to contemplate life. This is an act that is encouraged within the inner realms, as all there know the need to cogitate, not over the challenges, but their reactions to the challenges. They also spend time alone to contemplate how much they have, thanking creation forces and Creator for their journeys. It is more difficult here on this planet, many may exclaim. No, we tell you no, categorically not. How many cannot appreciate the budding of a flower, the salty wind blown on the face by the sea. The evaporating heat within a dessert scene rising from the ground like an oasis of new possibilities. Only those in depth of despair cannot view some form of creation with the reverence it deserves. We say to you that even those under terrible duress and lives of poverty are able to give thanks for the smallest thing. It again makes us question societal norms of allowing such situations in the first place. If a country belongs to no man, why are there so many wars over lands? Greed, my dear friends, greed of man. This is contemplated within the next chapter. Many reading this may hide behind their hands at reading such text, but all of you, bar a few, are accountable in one way or another for greed and greed of the lands, just as many of your forefathers were and you yourselves, through different incarnational experiences.

Back to fear. We see fears of things playing out regularly. By this we mean fear of the dark, fear of going out, fear of this or that animal, fear of becoming depressed, fear of anxiety, fear of going mad, fear for fear's sake. We wish to examine this concept, fear for fears sake. What does this mean? Fear for whose sake? The sake of not realising who you are? Fear you may wake up one day and begin to really live in the way in which Creator intended? Fear holds you back from this remembrance and in some way serves you, as you are able to justify actions due to the concept of fear. Fear that holds you back.

Of course, fear is a much more complex concept than we can possibly discuss within this text. Fear overlaps and derives from many other emotions you feel within the embodiment process. If we take lust, for example, lust can cause fears to arise. If we take the emotion lust, within the context of embodiment, we see it has many roots just as a root of a tree. Lust for wealth, lust that fuels sexual needs, lust for power. Lust caused the downfall of Lemuria and Atlantis, as the lust for power was so great. The lust of the elders is what we speak of. The lust to be better than the next person. The lust to show all that they had the right and only way to be close to Source. Such indoctrinations continue through many doctrines alive on this planet today. It interests us greatly how many such doctrines mention lust as being a negative force, which of course is true. Lust born from fear of course is what we are discussing within this context, and as such continues in a way, just as the times gone before, when we saw the downfall of great civilisations. Lust is cleared within this key set to help ensure that the recipients stand fully in their power as Creator beings. Lust born from fear is never a good attribute. Lusting after an experience is also worth a mention. Lust towards another in a committed relationship is never wrong in the eyes of Source, as this is the way of procreation. Lust towards many for self-gratification is, however, born from fear. The fear of not being loved. The eternal search for love in this way remains detrimental to the soul, as it gives away some soul essence and therefore love of the self. Love of the self cannot be underestimated. If we return you to chapter fifteen, we come to an understanding that the way in which you love yourself has much to do with your ability to shine and share your light with the world. When you love yourself, you truly know who you are, and that is a child of Creator, creating magical futures for all who you meet. So, we say lust through fear must go, as must self-depreciation, another grand reason why someone may lust in the first place. Self-depreciation differs somewhat from self-love, as self-depreciation includes emotional shame. This is the second key we offer you within this set.

Self-depreciation and self-deceit are contained within the key set known as 'the biggest blocks.' Self-depreciation, how many of you belittle yourselves. This differs somewhat from self-judgement, as self-depreciation goes deeper than this. It's embroiled with shame and shame is an emotion that serves no soul. What is shame? Shame is hoist upon you from outside experiences, shame is a judgement from society and others. Shame is a feeling which you digest, like too many rich tea biscuits, it sits heavy in your stomach, on your shoulders and within your soul. Shame for who you love, man or woman, it matters not to Source.

Let us state that what really matters is that you love with compassion. You love without judgement, you love without regret and you love with joy. Joy like taking in the essence of a waterfall pouring into a sunny cove, gleaming in the light. Joy like the dance of two lovers underneath the stars on a clear, crisp night. The child-like joy of a five-year-old riding a bike for the first time without their stabilisers. Joy. It matters not how you view it, as it goes beyond an experience or a sight. Joy is a feeling. Joy is a feeling that is able to course through your veins. When truly living in the light, with remembrance of who you are, this is how you can expect to live every day in joy.

There has been too little joy within much of your realm, for many, many centuries. Source decrees that this joy will return to your realm, the joy of standing in the love light of Creator. The sound of Om, the sound of creation vibrating through your veins. Before this becomes a real possibility, it is highly important that past issues, as many as possible, are cleared from your energy field. We remind you again that what is truly ascension is the rise in consciousness, back to the essence of love and light. This was the message of many masters. Fact. Who reading this, no matter what belief, can stand and dispute that this is not the basis of many of your religious beliefs. The rise back to love through being, expressing and acting from a place of love without fear, anger, judgement, regret, self-depreciation, deceit and shame.

So, let us view now how such self-depreciation may play out within your energy field. Let us all stop for a moment and put this book down and consider the last time you patted yourself on the back for a job well done. Now count how many times you have stopped and done this within the year, or the decade. It is this which we muse over within the higher echelons. Within the inner spheres, self-praise is practised daily and discussed with much glee. Self-praise is not something that derives from the ego, which of course it may. Self-praise is something that descends from the knowing of who you are, part of Creator. It is never wrong to joyfully express the good deeds you have done. Self-praise from ego is, however, a very different thing. Self-praise from ego causes resentment within others and it is not this of which we speak. The lack of self-praise of course affects your self-worth, and we remind you that if you cannot see the gifts you bring from your embodiment, how can others? We do not feel the need to delve deeper into this construct as we believe many of you grasp the facts presented here. So, we move swiftly on to the last key in this set which is the lack of joy you find within the embodiment process.

We are often astounded, or at least a little surprised, at the lack of joy which you find yourselves. Again, this is without judgement, as we understand many of the hardships you have faced within this realm of existence through many embodiment processes, of which of course many of you have no memory. Joy is the supreme gift from Creator, that and the everlasting love that vibrates from the very heart of creation. We have discussed some simple joys you may experience but we offer this key to clear up the lack of joy you felt from many of the embodiment experiences. We understand that when you returned to embodiment from the esoteric environment, you had many great plans. Plans that would teach you, but also give you great joy. Why do you think you chose to incarnate again and again? So you could do better next time and live with greater joy and love, to see the beauty in the smallest thing. So you could experience the way the sun made you feel alive on a summer's day. So you could resonate with the bird song with joy in dewy misty morns. So you could feel the hug of your friends as they wish you goodbye, till next time you may meet to while away many an hour. This is joy of which we speak. We wish for you to capture many joyous moments this life has to offer, this embodiment that you did so choose. We wish to awake you from the slumber and clear your eyes from the misty haze that has blocked you for so long in to seeing the beauty on your planet. Source, Creator, has deemed this and so we offer this key to reconnect you with the planet on which you reside, so you may live with joy within this realm of existence. We offer you this key with discernment and it is discernment we wish to explore within the next chapter, as discernment or the lack of discernment holds many back from joyous experience. So, we introduce the next set of keys in the hope that choices will be made wisely, with discernment, so joy may return to your realm in all its glory.

Earthly Intolerance Key Set

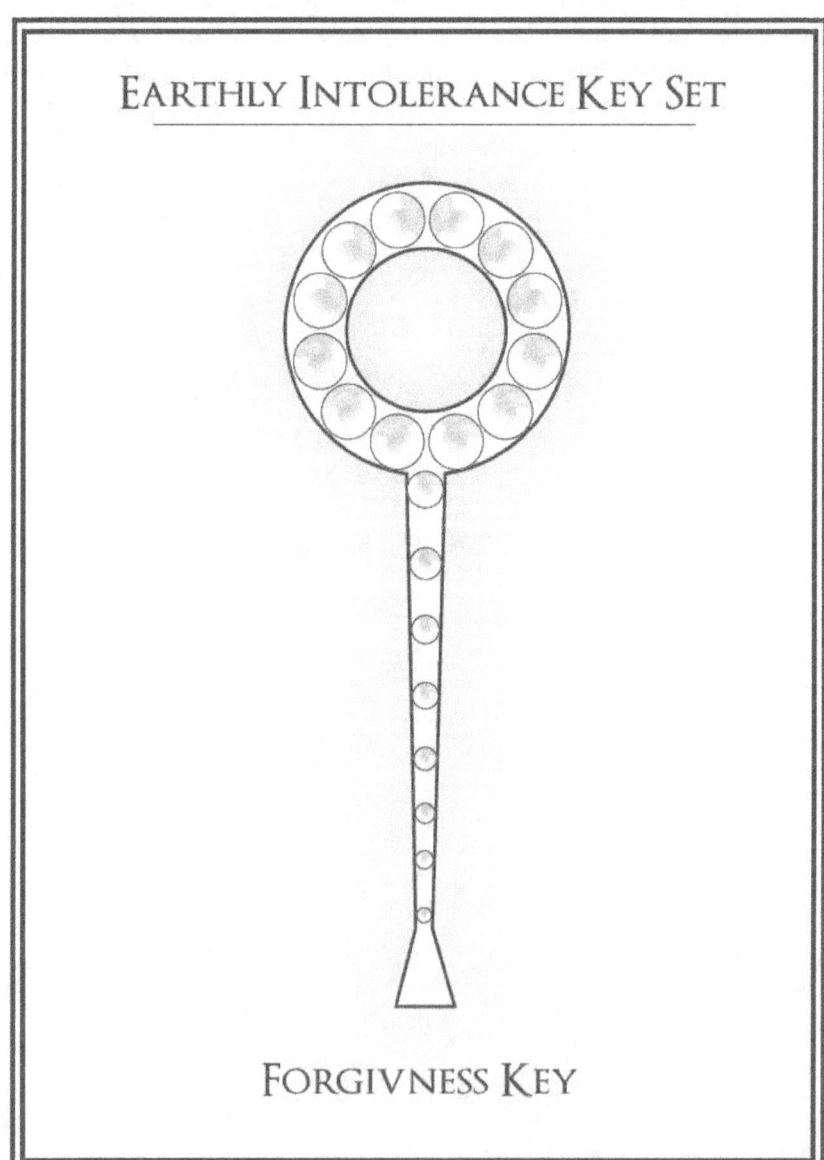

Forgivness Key

Chapter 19

Discernment, Choices and The Keys

The final key set we wish to introduce in depth is the one surrounding discernment. Discernment, what a word. It is the meaning of the word we wish you all to devour, like a bowl of hot soup on a cold and frosty night. Discernment gives a soul the ability to act in certain ways, ways that are in line with the higher realms of light. Were we all to act with not only discernment but integrity, as covered within previous chapters, the world in which you live would be a very different place. Everyone would be considering the highest good of all, including themselves. What does it truly mean to discern? It means that you are able to decipher light from dark, by this we mean darker paths and undesirable choices, and act with the highest reverence for all whom you come across.

So, within this set we offer the key of discernment, the key of choices and the key to a way to find yourself living with much patience. This key set is aptly named the key set that offers a possibility of perception. By this we refer to how you perceive certain ideologies and states, and Creator offers a new way to be in the world, when not of it. All of you are in the world, but not of it, as you are of everything, just as everything is of you. This is a complex perception, and by this we state you are all part of Creator, creating experiences so the light may shine brighter than any of you could possibly imagine within this sphere of existence. These words hope to shake a cellular memory or two, of the light that you all hold within your hearts and minds. So, these keys we offer you at this time, come as part of a totalitarian whole. A whole package to enlightenment back to the love light of Creator and creation, so you may live simply with more joy in your hearts, greater compassion within your souls, and this in part awakens others to live likewise. We have discussed the domino effect of the ascension process and how this effect needed and needs to be carefully monitored. We now state that the time is nigh for many dominoes to topple, as such new healing modalities are reintroduced to your realm. We have stated Creator has spoken, and many shifts are taking place that often go unseen. So, we continue now to discuss discernment, and so you will not feel hard done by as we draw near the close of this book, we offer you another little ditty to enliven your soul.

Discernment. Discernment, there is a name. A name the queen hadn't heard of, as she sat on her throne. She wasn't discerning, not in the least, she let in every man, animal and beast. She didn't discern between this and between that, and this alas is where she fell flat. Flat on her haunches, flat in her reign, flat in the way she did her business again, and again.

She let in the scoundrel, the storyteller, the beast. The beast of the night that gobbled her feast. She let in the fortune teller, telling of fates, she didn't take heed that this was all fake. She took in the mindsets from here and from there, without being mindful they laid her out bare. Bare in the way she distributed wealth, bare in the way, as they scourged through her house.

If only she had asked for some help from upstairs, they wouldn't have been able to leave her house bare. Creator is able to offer such gifts, gifts of discernment with all that you do. Gifts of discernment for me and for you. Gifts of discernment for that queen this day, so her fate was able to change in various ways. She was able to clear up the scoundrels and thieves. She was able to discern between the things she did seek. Seek to hear about her fate, and connect with Creator and know what was fake. She was able to discern whose hand she should wed, and put other suitors far away from her bed.

She was then free to distribute her wealth to those in need who hadn't a house. She was able to help those in great need, so the scoundrels calmed down and weren't coming from greed. As their past had been dire for many lives to be sure, the queen was able to help open the door. The door to a new life, full of the joys and the laughter, the lack of which causes strife for many moons after.

So, we ask those of you reading this text to consider discernment with all that you do, even when buying a pair of new shoes. What do we mean by this statement you may well ask? We mean by this statement, have those shoes been involved with unethical tasks. The tasks that we speak of are the labour of love, were there sweat shops involved or were they made with true love? This is the choice we face in this modern age. The choices you make can dig a grave, a grave of despair for some certain folk, that keeps them enslaved in the lives that they make. So choices are so important, you see. Choices affect not just you but all far and wide, so all may be dipping their toes in the golden tide. The golden tide that is life, in the way that makes your earth quake, not with despair but with light and love that makes your earth shake. The choices we make.

Choices now there is a thing. Choices affect all, as it is within the choices we may discuss aspects of the great Universal Laws. Going back to cause and effect, actions and reactions, have they not all stemmed from the choices made? Choices judged good or bad, choices deemed right and wrong, choices for the highest good of all or at the detriment of many. When deliberated within such contexts, we see choices affect all and many lives have been halted, disrupted, endangered, belittled or judged because of such choices. So, we offer this set of keys so that the choices you make after receiving are in alignment with the highest vibration of all which, of course, is love. Choices. This key sounds so unimportant compared to many previous keys discussed, but we say to you it is one of the most important. If all within this realm made choices for the highest good of all, many wars, famines and such would cease to exist. So, it is with great joy that this set is encapsulated within the key sets. With choice of course comes patience, the final key of this set. Patience is required in all aspects of life and sits nicely within this set, as highest choices made with patience bring much joy and cause to celebrate. With patience, discernment and highest choices much of the world's problems could cease.

Patience springs from many past lives of rushing about and is tied up with survival, as you have all scrabbled to survive due to the choices you and many others made. If we take hierarchical structures of past noble men and women, we see that the choices they made were often not for the highest good of all, and they often impatiently made choices that affected many for their own gain. We see even today patience remaining an issue, and within many western societies road rage remains a fact on many of your roads. Mainly driven by fear, enveloped with anger states, but very much caught up with the inability to have the patience that is required to partake in such journeys. We of course state that many of the issues we have discussed within this book overlap with other differing states, and it would be naïve to assume that one key standing alone will fix all of the issues you face within your realm. However, the movement of energy from one key session can also not be underestimated, as Creator decides which issues are deemed the most important within the ceremony, and therefore what is received can only be for the highest good for all, not only the receiver but for those who they interact with. So, it is with much patience within the esoteric spheres that much of this text is written, as we fully acknowledge Rome wasn't built in a day. As such we state just as Rome wasn't, attitudes and emotions will not change overnight. It takes much work on one's self to fully live in, by and with, esoterically speaking, higher awareness states. This is the task many of you have ahead of you as the seasons ebb and wane and the years pass you by, we state again that Creator has decreed that great change will be upon you. It matters not how you clear the paths for future generations, it is just a fact that this will be so. Your history books will look back on this time in your history with disbelief that this could have ever been so. We remind you of times gone by when you first had the electric current lighting your homes, you were able to call someone across the country and tell them you were ok, you were able to travel through the skies with the greatest of ease. Do you suppose three hundred years before, any of you within that incarnation could foretell of the possibilities that exist today? We say to you, those reading this text, read it with an open mind. All is possible with belief in yourselves and others, the ability that great change in perception is possible. Many masters came to show you this way, the way of the light, and many hid such tales under a bushel believing only the great masters could do many of these great things. We again diplomatically state that you have the ability to master many aspects of that which was taught, regardless of religious doctrine.

So, we conclude this chapter by asking those reading this to take from it what you will and leave behind that which does not resonate, as it matters not to us if believed or not believed, only that great change is upon you and the struggles you have faced will become cleared. Creator's gift to you is ascension back towards the love light of creation. So, we offer the final chapter on the keys to tie up any loose ends, briefly discussing the last sets of keys in its wake. As we leave this journey of exploration into many emotional aspects and crosses you have born, we hope that you will have contemplated the way in which you wish to live your lives and the glory of all creation with all its aspects. The light and the dark, the ancestral patterns that have held you back and your journeys back to remembrance of who you truly are. As all and as one of you are part of Creator, the children of Source, with a light in your higher heart that will burn bright for eternity, remembered or not within this incarnational experience.

Divine Intentions Key Set

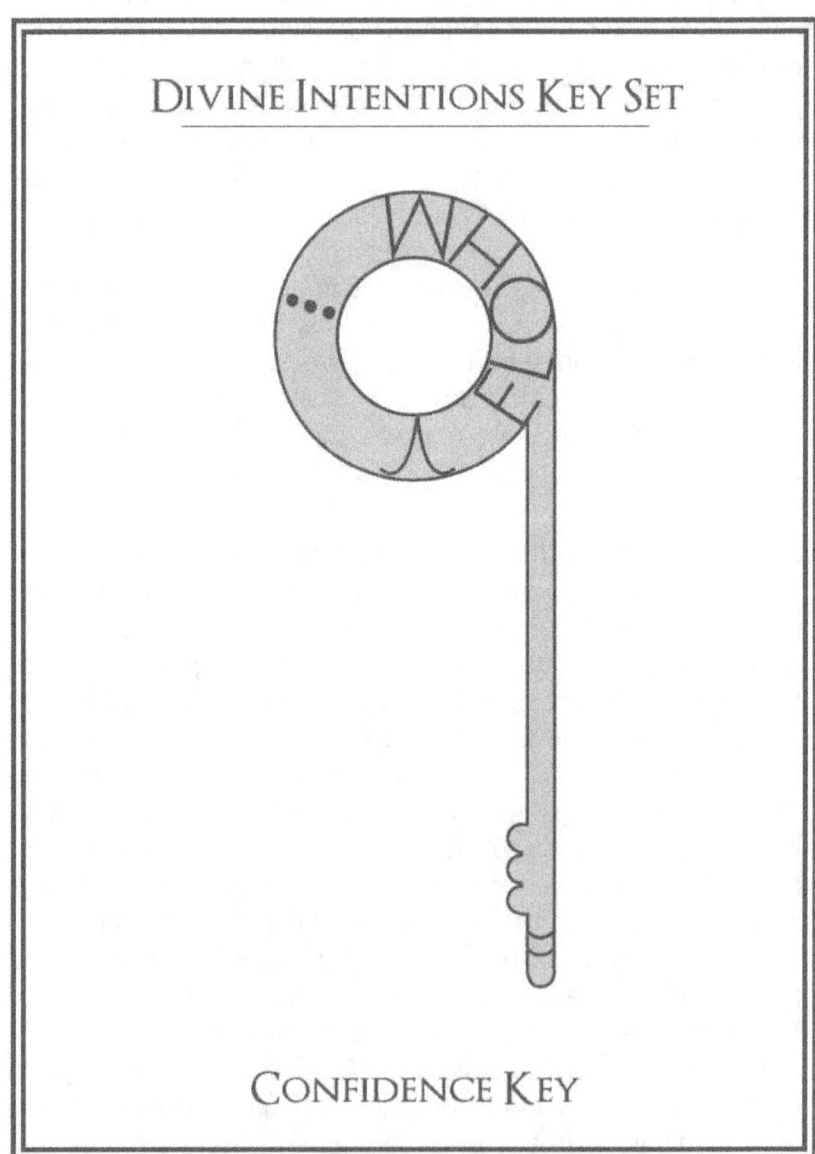

Confidence Key

Chapter 20

The Final Countdown and The Keys

We name this last chapter the final countdown and the keys, as we countdown now to the end of our teachings contained within this text. This leads us nicely into the summary of all we have taught, with the concluding chapter 'Marmite or honey?' We now discuss the final sets of keys we offer and do not wish, at this time, to go into great depth, as you have been taught, we hope, much within this body of texts. Many of the final sets are self-explanatory.

So, we offer the set of the healing arts in order to aid you heal many of your own issues you face in embodiment. We categorically state you are your own healers, and when it is time for you to leave the earthly plains this will be so, as you have predetermined it. This is part of the Universal Law of Creation that states 'your free will determines the time you return home.' We have discussed that this is never consciously concluded, as it would deter many from the journey they wished to undertake. The worry and fretting of the brow would be to tremendous at this time for you, or those you touch within embodiment to bear. We state that whichever way you decide to return home is the way you deemed fit for the lessons you, and those around, required within the incarnational experience you find yourselves. Many will claim no way, this cannot be so, and it is not our job to debate such choice as there are many ways to return to the kingdom of light. Many at this time may be filled with earthly anguish. We do not detract from such anguish, and wish that those reading this find some sort of peace within this text, as it is offered to you as a way of comfort.

So, you may know the eternity of existence. We recap that from atrocity, many societal changes are indeed founded for the good of many. This does not help the few that suffer in the moment that is deemed now, through having to endure the emotional responses such atrocious acts entail. This text may, in fact, be of little comfort and for this we apologise. We add such a serious topic as we do not wish to shy away from the very real incidences that impact greatly upon you within this realm. Failing to add this to the text would be unjust as we offer to aid you to clear many emotional responses that have held you back, we wish to say that this is not a cure for all ills, suffering and the darker routes some souls choose. It has been offered to you so that those that have resonance with what they read may change by whichever means they deem fit. This helps the masses awaken from their slumber. As more awaken there will be many less atrocities of which we speak, and you know to be true, have experienced or heard about. We offer these keys so that the planet may rise in the light like a great orange ball residing within the love light of creation. So back to the keys and the healing set.

We state that the first key within this set offers the healing of many issues that interrupt your energy field, aiding it to become free from dis-ease. We state the word dis-ease so that many can understand that it is emotional dis-ease that you feel when you suffer so. So we break the word dis-ease with a hyphen, so you, the reader, may understand this concept. The concept that you are not at ease when you suffer from disease states. We state again that you are the healer and as such healing comes from within, this key offers hope, as it clears beliefs that such inner healing is not possible and sets down a new resonance by calming the dis-ease that holds you back. We are not claiming that this will bring healing to specific sufferings, only that with a new ease, free from dis, combined with the clearing of other emotional set points, healing is possible. If we examine the meaning of 'dis' we understand that it has negative connotation, and in fact pertains to some disconnection of sorts.

It is possible to heal yourselves from within. This is a statement which we are sure will cause much debate. Many may throw this statement away with contempt, and that is also fine. Healing from within does not suit all, as it is a deep and sometimes emotional journey that may be required to reach such states of living dis-ease free. Compounded with this is the lessons you came here to experience, whether deemed great for self or those which you touch. So, we state that this key set does not claim to cure all ills. It just ignites a new attitude to the possibilities that surround you. The rest, they say, has many aspects that involve emotional and spiritual disconnect, and this would involve a whole new book!

We offer within this set the key that aids addictive patternings, those you brought in with you. It does not offer to clear the reason why you continue with addictive behaviours, as there may be many reasons for this. If we examine the lady who turned to drink in chapter eight, within the Universal Law of Resonance, we understand that some patterning may be passed down timelines and this can be cleared with this key. We offer this key within this set as such patterns cause much disease.

We also offer the key of divine possibility. This keys aids those in receipt to remain open to the possibilities that healing of self is possible. Creator works with the individual within this ceremony, clearing individual nuances that may affect healing potentials. It differs from the first key offered as it works with beliefs installed within you from many incarnational experiences. We decided not to go into great depth in regard to this set as we do not wish for you, the reader, to get caught up on a cure. It is within many of the keys sets that the answers lie to many dis-eases that are prevalent within the earthly realm. Many, unfortunately, are caused through societal injustices. We have explored this theory when debating the bubonic plague and state 'that many such dis-eases occur today due to the undue lack of care for others within your societies.' We again stress the need for those living in and with awareness, to utilise many healing methods to live free from dis-ease and in writing this we do not wish to condemn conventional tactics. We do state, however, that there are many ways to heal and this requires an open mind. We wish to discuss the keys within the context of dis-ease and state that when you clear up dis-eased states there is a greater prospect of self-healing. So, we offer the key set earthly intolerances in order for more dis-eased states to be transformed. The name speaks for itself.

'Earthly intolerances'; how they hold you back. We name these as jealously, betrayals and rejections and forgiveness. The term intolerance derives from the Latin word intolerantia, to be out of balance, not moving forward, not bearing the deeds perceived as 'done to you.' We say to you that the deeds done to you, you have done to many others over many lives. Do not live in false the pretence that you have never perpetrated such acts. The reason so many of you hide your heads under the bushel simply stems from a lack of awareness of your many and often turbulent incarnations. We say this is how you planned it, the lack of remembrance of who you were, or have been. To face such truths takes courage and we respect those of you that have started to examine these parts of your soul's experiences. This is truly how you ascend, and whilst we do not wish you to dwell on past times, we wish you now to clear the emotional baggage you incarnated with in the here and now. This will give you such freedoms, my friends. This will truly make the earth quake beneath your feet. Not with trepidation for all your tomorrows but living in the glory of the todays. This is the wish of Creator, and there are many unseen master angels and guides that, esoterically speaking, are waiting in the wings to aid you on this journey of self-discovery.

So, we offer the self-explanatory set of these keys that we

chat about so that clearing the emotional responses to such perceived injustices forges a new path ahead. We discuss that when they are gone they are gone, no longer requiring the need to be repeated within this realm of existence and reality in which you find yourselves. You may, of course, always choose to experience this at another point in time from another view point. We say 'point in time' as loosely as possible, as time is irrelevant, my dear friends. It is in the here and now you need to concentrate within your journeying. The here and now, whilst making your own glorious futures free from such encumbering emotional responses.

We wish to briefly discuss the concept of forgiveness as within many of your religious constructs much a 'to do' has been made. We say that the hardest person to forgive is yourselves. We do not in saying this exonerate the need for you to forgive others, as all this burning anger, remunerations and what ifs eats away at your true identity, blocking the way to the light. We start by discussing the forgiveness of self as dear ones, this is where many such attitudes lay, of course dormant, in the subconscious mind. By this we discuss the lack of remembrance of your past deeds, and so the term 'to turn the other cheek' was, in fact, quite correct as within this phrase there was a hidden meaning. In saying this, it does denote that the primary cheek holds many stories of the acts that you yourself have committed. When viewed in this way and fully appreciated, it becomes much easier to forgive others. Within the ceremonies there is no need to trawl through all the journeying experiences where such acts have been committed. Creator is able to clear such responses in a blink of an eye. If a story rears its head in such a session, it is simply a reminder that you, the recipient, is required to remember to aid you on the path back to enlightenment. The final and truly glorious set we wish to discuss is that of divine intention, as this set clears the path to walk through life in a much enhanced way.

The final set is that of truth and honour and beauty and

confidence. This set is known as divine intentions. Who does not wish to live with all these attributes? Who does not wish to awaken and start a new day with such divine intentions running through their veins? No one but a fool. We are not calling those walking the darker paths foolish, as they are indeed on their own journey of remembrance, as are all souls. We are saying that their spark has not ignited within their bosoms sufficiently to be able to contemplate such attributes, and we live in the knowledge that one day it indeed will. Whether this takes millions of millennia to accomplish is not in question, we discuss this within the context of the eternity of all things. We have previously established this construct throughout this text. We use the term 'only a fool' with the enlightened masses. This is truly the way in which you all wish to live, not only with love, joy, integrity and with discernment, but with truth, honour, beauty and confidence. That makes each day within the incarnational experience a treasure trove of wondrous adventures. It's like running freely through the blooming meadows of existence, seeing the beauty within the trees and the animals that adorn the landscapes. This is not stated with an idealistic, utopian set point as we understand the hardships of your lands. We discuss it in this way so your individual soul experience may begin to experience such joys of the eternal fruits of their labours. Such labours have been gained through many lifetimes and now, back to the grand uncloaking my friends. To the remembrance of who you are and a new way to live free from the past constraints that did hold you back so. Many journeys of the soul who made you who you are, who made you learn and grow. Never forsaken, esoterically speaking, often waiting in the wings for the spark to reunite with the creational tides of love and light.

So, in concluding this chapter we again remind you that such journeying to remembrance leads into group consciousness and raises the planet back to the vibration of love light, of which we so often speak. The fact that we are all one, as Creator created everything, and everything leads back to

Creator in its own unique way, must never be forgotten. We finally discuss, in regards to the keys, that there are some sacred keys that remain firmly for the use by The Key Keepers and ascended masters. They aid certain souls with specific needs, of course they really are part of Creator's gifts to you and as such truly only belong to Creator as everything does. It is truly Creator who decides if such keys are utilised within the sacred ceremony space. So, we now round up this book by asking you was this Marmite or honey to your ears and senses? This is indeed the title of the concluding chapter.

The Biggest Blocks Key Set

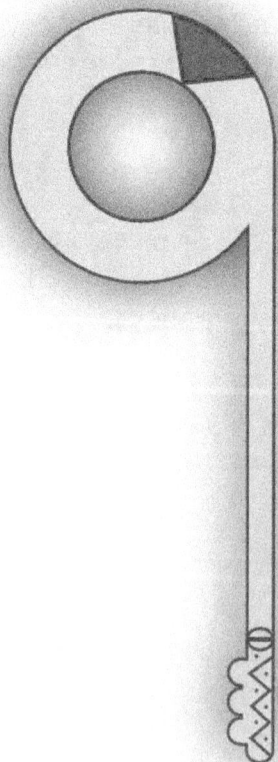

Self Deprecation & Self Deceit Key

Chapter 21

Marmite or Honey?

Marmite or honey, whichever it is fine. If it ignites some remembrance of who you are, if it tickles a nerve or two, then we say the ascended masters and this book have done their job. We understand how it may be beyond comprehension to some that they have walked this mother planet many times. It may have incited some anger as it may conflict with mainstream views. We only ask that some thought is given to the possibility of these facts. We encourage you to debate and take from this text what you will, and that which doesn't resonate, leave it behind like a discarded plimsole. After all, that is why you were given the gift of free will. This concept has been woven throughout this text and we hope that you may continue to use your free will with the resonance of love, for yourself this is most important and partly the point of such writings. We hope such great love will dominate your interactions with others you meet along your journeying into the unknown realms of your future existences. We wish you to think long and hard about the dear mother planet on which you reside and respect the lands that none of you truly own. We hope many religious fractions may join together to become one giant ball of love for the supreme Creator, as the Creator loves you all in such a way, with the upmost regard. These are all our hopes.

We know, however, that ascension is upon you. Known or unknown it matters not, Creator has spoken, and your existence will change. We have informed you of this fact and we now sum it up nicely with one of our tales within a tale.

There once was a planet it beamed out a light, not always

bright on a clear starry night. The planet named earth, it's where you reside, this planet has much beauty and peace deep inside. The people upon it, restricted by greed, had blocked up the lines it is time to set free, the restrictions that have kept all from dancing with glee. The planet is part of creation, you see.

There is much help above you that many can't see, we have discussed the angels who are there to help thee, we hope you agree. We discussed ascended masters who wait in the wings, to bring a whole amount of unified love in, and aid you all to live like your kings. We have discussed Laws of the Universe that need to be taught, to your children, without second thought. We hope you explore them in greater depth this is true, as they aid you to appreciate all that you do.

We have discussed many concepts that hold you all back. Like loving yourself, and that is a fact. We have explored the reason for this and for that. It may lay in your past, and this alas, beats you up like a bad weather forecast. We have offered solutions to all this self-doubt, the keys are on offer to clear up your house! There are many tools on offer, upon your plane, don't limit yourself, if you do it's in vain. Keep up the work on clearing your past, the joy you receive from this will be vast. You will enthuse others to join you, you see, then all of you may once again join the glee. The planet will rise up from its slumber, and all of you will feel the love of Creator, of this there's no doubt or blunder. The love from Creator will shake up your house, and bring you great merriment into to your lighthouse.

The universe is vast, believe it or not! It's time to move on now not live in the past. At one time you all believed the earth was flat, and walking across it, you would eventually go splat. We are here to inform you that things they progress, and beliefs they can change, and this is our keynote address. We do not wish to digress from the importance of life-given gifts, the beauty of nature, and this can cause shifts. Shifts in awareness, why this is true. That is the point for me and for you.

The shifts in awareness that make you rise from your slumber and see existence without all the unbalanced cumber. Just open your eyes to the magic out there, the magic of creation, if you do dare.

Timelines can shift like a tree in the breeze, so all of you can be living with new shiny leaves, without feeling the squeeze of the depressing wheeze. All timelines are, is a consciousness shift, that will definitely make you live with a new-found bliss. Vibrations around you then they shall rise out of the clouds, so peace and tranquillity may not pass you by. Back to the sound that resonates through the plains of existence called Om. Back to the Source where you all originate from.

We hope we have warned you of the power of the keys, they can be misused so we hope you take heed. They must be used with the upmost care and respect, as all energy work must be and this you must check. So act with discernment in all that you do, if you do not it will make you feel blue, and this you can be sure of, you don't want to do.

When manifesting make sure it's for good. The answer doesn't lie in others' opinion; this is not for the good. The answers are found from way deep inside, so you may once again ride that crimson tide, back to whom you are truly deep inside. There is a spark way down there in your souls, the spark of Creator, just wanting to shine with glorious majestic intent that is truly divine. We hope you took heed from the old lady in the shoe and be careful what you wish for whatever you do. Make sure of wise choices that are always for good, don't be wearing a misguided hood.

We sum up this tale now and thank you for your time, which is held in this moment all that's divine. Remember your records are held for your good, so you may make sense of the walks in the woods. You may make sense of the joy that life brings and clear up the traumas that incarnational experiences brings. Lessons are kept for your highest good, it's the emotions that surround them that do you no good. So we sum up quite nicely, and give thanks for the keys, gifted from Creator with timely intent. To aid the ascension, to help all to transcend back to the glory and beauty again.

The final paragraph is reminding all of the unseen beings waiting in the wings to aid your journeying, with special thanks to Lord Melchizedek and the 'Order of Melchizedek', without whom this book would not have been produced in such an eloquent way. I thank my dear friend whole heartily for sharing this knowledge, and this comes with the understanding that a few years ago I would never have believed such possibilities could or did exist. It is my expressed wish many of you reading this will find your way back towards the love light of Creator, and you as Creator beings may stand within your power and exert a higher vibrational frequency than you ever felt possible. The vibration of love, for the good of all that reside upon and within this plane. I thank you for reading, may your journeys be filled with grace and ease.

Useful Websites

I enclose a list of useful websites in case any of you are drawn to book a session with the keys, or indeed are drawn to train in this art. My website can be viewed by visiting:

www.starlighttherapies.com

I included these other websites that pertain to other healing modalities that I have mentioned within the foreword. Carol Stacey has since retired, but all information can be found by visiting Neshla Avey's site. She has taken over the running of this beautiful modality. Carol's books and CDs can be found here:

www.neshlaavey.com

Susan Kennard offers various healing modalities including inner child trauma therapy and singing light language and is well known for her work within the healing arts. Please visit:

www.susankennard.co.uk

www.singingfromthelight.co.uk

Thanks to Philippa King for her great teachings and her online programme that aided many shifts in blocks to success and aided with the building of a healing business. She can be found at:

www.shinethriveacademy.com

The front cover of the book has been created by a highly talented artist named Gary Bennett. His work can be viewed by visiting:

www.garybennettpictures.co.uk

Customised website design and management by Simon Hampton. Visit:

www.hwms.co.uk

www.ingramcontent.com/pod-product-compliance
Lightning Source LLC
LaVergne TN
LVHW051521070426
835507LV00023B/3224